Can. aut of print

MW01687440

HE SAW WITH OTHER EYES
Stories from the Cariboo

HE SAW WITH OTHER EYES
Stories from the Cariboo

by Todd Lee

The Caitlin Press
Prince George, British Columbia
1992

Copyright © 1992 by Todd Lee

All rights reserved. No part of this book may be reproduced in any form by any means without the written permission of the publisher, except by a reviewer, who may quote passages in a review.

The Caitlin Press
P.O. Box 2387, Station B
Prince George, B.C. V2N 2S6
Canada

Caitlin Press would like to acknowledge the financial support of the Canada Council and British Columbia Cultural Fund.

Canadian Cataloguing in Publication Data

Lee, Todd, 1924-
He Saw With Other Eyes

ISBN 0-920576-37-0

1. Cariboo (B.C. : Regional district)—History.
2. Lee, Todd, 1924- 3. Cariboo (B.C. : Regional district)—Biography. 4. Clergy—British Columbia —Cariboo (Regional district)—Biography. I. Title.
FC3845.C3Z49 1992 971.1 7504 092 C92-091505-1
F1089.C3L43 1992

Cover design and illustrations by Gaye Hammond

Printed in Canada

Contents

Introduction

You had to live in Williams Lake in the 1950s to appreciate the atmosphere of a dusty cow town that was about to meet its destiny as an important city. But at that time it was poised somewhere between a railroad whistle stop and a town with a possible future.

We were into indoor plumbing, and although the odd outhouse was still around, there were definite signs of improvement. The first cement sidewalks made their appearance, dotted with parking meters on the main street. We acquired a village hall, curling rink, health unit, library, and a chain store.

Sleek new Budd cars replaced the old steam locomotives on the PGE line and a new airport was started nine miles from town and the old one turned into a housing sub-division.

Williams Lake still held the record as the largest cattle shipping point in the province, but lumbering became the major industry. With it came people to hew the logs and people to man the necessary supporting businesses and services. New stores, modern garages, motels, and restaurants sprang up.

It was a busy, exciting era in the growth of the city, and the once familiar sobriquet of "Willie's Puddle" disappeared from use.

It was a town made up of colorful characters and colorful stories of people on the move. They were mostly hard working, hard playing folk, but despite their idiosyncrasies they were warm, hospitable, and honest. The kind of people you liked to call friends.

Some of their stories have been preserved by United Church minister Todd Lee who lived for some time in the Williams Lake of the 1950s. Reading these parables of early life in our city gives you an insight of life in the Cariboo forty years ago.

If you were unfortunate enough not to have experienced life in our town back in the 50s, these gentle stories will emphasize what you missed.

Clive Stangoe
Retired publisher,
Williams Lake Tribune

Coming Home

It was 4:30 p.m. on the 28th of June 1956 when I drove into Williams Lake, a young minister appointed to his first pastoral charge. To say that I was nervous was to put it lightly. No more studies, no more examinations, no more theses. Was I up to it? Only time would tell.

The first thing I discovered was a pleasant surprise—paved streets. When I left the Cariboo eight years before, Williams Lake streets, like the Cariboo highway were gravel and subject to all the whims of the elements. I'd be getting stuck trying to pull away from the curb on the town's main street.

To some extent, I had been prepared for the second discovery. The old United Church and manse on Oliver Street were gone—certainly no loss as far as the manse was concerned. A relic of the days when old Dr. McKinnon, in the back seat of an equally ancient car, toured the Cariboo—chauffeured by his wife—it had only after World War II boasted of indoor plumbing.

Actually, both the old church and manse were still in

town . . . just not in their old places. Both had become private residences, the church moved to Cameron Street, and the manse out to Glendale. Glendale, too, was new. When I had left for university, it had been a motley collection of rough cabins and shacks and was called after its onetime owner, Smedleyville.

I made my way first to the home of long-time church members, George and Elna, and picked up a key to the new manse located at the corner of Third Avenue and Cameron Street, across from the arena. Around the corner was the church hall that also the sanctuary for St. Andrews until finances improved enough to warrant building the church next door. Unfortunately, the church was never built.

During those long years it took me to prepare for my chosen career, we had lived in premises spartan in the extreme. I recall one terrible winter in a duplex off Vancouver's False Creek, and and another in a drafty shack—with a million dollar view—at Wardner in the east Kootenays. The three-bedroom manse in Williams Lake was a mansion in comparison. I wondered what other kinds of changes—maybe less pleasant—I would find.

I turned the key and walked into our new home. The kitchen was bright and modern; the living-room comfortably furnished, opening onto a dining area. I pulled the drapes and looked across to the arena and Highways Department yard. A street person moved along the far side. As I watched, he lifted a plank and pulled out a mickey of rum. Well, some things in Williams Lake had not changed.

Because I would spend the next four weeks directing boys' programs at the Cariboo Youth Camp, my wife and our two children had remained at the coast with their grandparents. We had applied to adopt a third child and had been advised by our social worker that placement was imminent. There was so much to do. Perhaps it was just as well to be alone for a few weeks, though I missed my family dreadfully.

I made a cup of coffee and wandered over to the church to explore. My study was upstairs over the entry hall. I was surprised to find the study shelves well stocked with books. Not until I made my next move did I realize that young ministers collect books with interesting titles, but find them useless as reference works. When it was my turn to vacate the study, I would leave more books than I found.

My exploration took me next to the pulpit. I looked down at the rows of empty pews and was suddenly struck with the enormity of the task before me. Nine years earlier, I had stood before the Presbytery of the Cariboo and consented to be received as a candidate for the ministry. Now I had come full circle. The Settlement Committee, in its wisdom, had sent me back to serve my home church. Was I equal to the task?

My predecessor had left a map of the Williams Lake Pastoral Charge, showing the boundaries of the area for which I was responsible. I stood in front of it and identified the preaching points in rural areas outside of Williams Lake: Lac La Hache, 100 Mile House and Bridge Lake to the south, Miocene, Horsefly and Black Creek to the east, Macalister to the north and all of the Chilcotin to the west. For a long moment I felt a sense of panic. It must be 10 000 square miles! How could I possibly cover all that territory?

Then I remembered: these were *my* kind of people. I could understand their needs, their fears, their aspirations, for I, too, was a product of the vast reaches of the Cariboo. I was home here, although I had learned what it was like to be an outsider.

While studying at Union College at the University of British Columbia, I served a term as Christian Education Director at St. Andrews-Wesley United, a large downtown church. I had never felt so uncomfortable and inadequate as I had among those cosmopolitan, urban people. Here in the Cariboo, I was at home.

I arrived in Williams Lake on the eve of its most important festival: the annual stampede. Clouds of dust hung over the rodeo grounds as bucking stock was readied for the events. Tents blossomed on the hills below town as natives from all points of the compass moved in for the duration of the Stampede.

Suddenly I had an impish idea: suppose I signed up to ride a bronc? I grinned as I pictured the headline that might appear in the local paper:

NEW PADRE RIDES BRONC

Now bronc riding wasn't a credit course at seminary, but this was bronc riding country, and I had 'forked' some pretty skookum buckers in my ranching days. Then I sobered as I pictured another possible headline:

NEW PADRE BREAKS LEG AT RODEO GROUNDS

Fortunately, perhaps, when I bounced the idea off a church elder, it was suggested to me in firm tones than riding broncs was inappropriate behaviour for a minister of the United Church. Darn! I would have to win my laurels in less exciting ways, such as thumping the pulpit.

What mattered now was that I had a task to begin and an exciting role to play. For eight years I had gathered tools for the work that I would be called upon to do. I was ready. But most of all, I was back in the Cariboo where I had grown up. I was home.

Heigh ho, Come to the Fair

Second only to the annual stampede was the Cariboo Fall Fair and Cattle Sale. This three day event drew participants from every corner of the Cariboo, cattle buyers from all the major packing companies, and spectators from as far away as Vancouver and Edmonton.

Weeks before the event, herds of cattle began to move from their holding pastures deep in the Chilcotin on a leisurely course towards the cattle yards at Williams Lake. Beef sold by the pound, so to conserve those precious pounds, cowboys moved the herds slowly, sometimes only six or seven miles a day. Night pasture was leased from friendly ranch spreads along the way.

In the days immediately before the Fair and Cattle Sale, the roads and hillsides leading to the stockyards at the end of the Lake were a rolling, lowing mass of cattle, bound for their last roundup. Most of the cattle were red and white Herefords, lending bright tints to autumn colors.

At the stockyards, cowboys and yard helpers sorted the cattle with a master plan totally incomprehensible to me. They matched groups by age, weight and gender, then separated them into pen lots that would make sense to the auctioneer and cattle buyers.

Across from the stockyards were show buildings that housed other exhibits at the Fair: garden produce, flower arrangements, arts and crafts of every sort and shape. There were balloons and games and treats for the kids, many of whom, mounted on horses, raced back and forth through the grounds. Dogs barked, horses whinnied, cattle bawled, cowboys shouted. Everyone was caught up in the excitement of the Fall Fair and Cattle Sale.

What was the role of a one-time cowboy turned cleric in the midst of all this excitement? To be honest, my status was reduced to that of go-for. Let me explain.

The hard-working Women's Auxiliary to St. Andrew's United Church by tradition took on the task of serving meals to the Foregoers. This was their major fund-raiser of the year, and without its successful operation there would be little maintenance or improvements done on the church and manse.

Like the management of the Cattle Sale, the organization behind this task of feeding the multitudes was equally unfathomable to me. Weeks of planning went into it. Loads of supplies went in the back door, and, by some metamorphosis created by many willing hands in the kitchen, came out in the form of mouth-watering beef stew and hot apple pie.

My position was on the supply side, making many trips uptown for groceries from McKenzie's Store, meat from Hawker's Meat Market, and freshly peeled potatoes from Famous Cafe. Strangely enough, I felt very useful in this role. Here was a task that showed immediate results.

There were lulls in my duties, however, and it was during these breaks that I had time to sit in the stands and observe the action. Hundreds of cattle changed hands with the simple uplift of a bidding card. The staccato repertoire of auctioneer Matt Hassen succeeded in milking the last possible dollar from poker- faced buyers at the ringside.

Occasionally there was humour. In the midst of this wholesale marketing, I was surprised to see the handlers usher a single animal into the ring.

"Now, here's something different for you, ladies and gentlemen," Hassen quipped, "A *hermaphrodite.* Yes, that's right. Doesn't matter if you can't spell it, you can still bid! Now, what am I offered for this two-holer? Should be worth twice as much, hey?"

There was much laughter but not much bidding. This genetic oddity went for less than the average lot. Buyers appeared wary of an "either-or" specimen of beef.

I was not completely new to the process of cattle sales. As a curious ten-year-old, I had perched on the fence at Enterprise Station to watch and listen while a sale took place. I remember a buyer looking at a pen of mature cows, then calling out, "A cent and a half a pound?" The neighbor owner called back, "Good enough."

At the price agreed upon back in 1935, a good cow would bring $15. When my brother and I sold our last beef in 1949, a mature cow brought $150. The prices I heard in the sale ring in 1956 seemed almost too good to be true. Still, I didn't see great joy on the faces of ranchers. A sale was a sale and if money didn't roll in as fast as it rolled out, well, there's always next year.

The Cariboo rancher is usually given more to hope than to enthusiasm. He knows that if there is a bumper crop of hay it will rain all summer and mould it; if the sun shines on his harvesting efforts and he has hay to sell, no other rancher will need it; and if prices are high it will be the year *after* he sold down his herd to pay for high priced equipment. He knows in his heart, though, that next year everything will come together and he'll make a killing. And in spite of his grousing, he'll enjoy it.

Lost in memories of years gone by, I was jarred back to the present back to the present by a summons from the dining hall: the supply of potatoes was running low. My clerical chariot was tethered behind the dining hall, waiting for me to sit high in the saddle and race for the Famous Cafe. I laid a trail of dust all the way to town and back again.

It was at this point that I came near to altering the history of Canada. Perhaps I was concentrating too fully on the urgency of my mission, maybe too much on a boy weaving towards me on a bike. In any case, I was caught by surprise when a man emerged suddenly from behind a stack of baled hay and strode onto the road without pausing to look. Even as my foot stabbed for the brake, I recognized the Honourable Davie Fulton, soon to become Justice Minister of Canada (or a corpse).

As someone quipped, "God is good and the devil not half bad!" The boy chose that moment to swerve away on the right, giving me precious maneuvering room. Through a cloud of dust I caught a glimpse of a startled scowl and heard an epithet most unbecoming to a minister of the Crown.

No harm was done. Davie Fulton dusted off his white suit and continued on his way, I delivered the potatoes to God's faithful servants in the Cattle Sale Kitchen, and life unfolded as it should. However, as I relaxed over a cool drink and allowed my heart beat to come back to normal, I contemplated the headline that might have emblazoned the next Tribune:

CARIBOO CLERIC RUNS DOWN CABINET MINISTER

High Noon in a Cow-town Court

It was one of those occasions when many of the folk of Williams Lake get together around groaning richly-laden tables in the Elk's Hall. As the newest minister in town, I was to pronounce a blessing over the culinary delights and the women whose hands had prepared them. I was seated at the head table, near the front of the packed room. I turned to introduce myself to the gentleman on my left and then the lady on my right. When she told me her name, something rang a bell in the recesses of my memory.

"Haven't we met before?" she asked pleasantly.

"I'm not sure . . . ." I replied. "You *do* look familiar. It might have been before I left for university." Then it came back to me. We *had* met before, years before . . . only that time she was riding a horse. My mind faded back over the years . . . .

. . . There comes a time when feeding cows on a wild hay meadow ranch loses much of its thrill. Such a time came to my brother and me in March of 1947. Three feet of snow lay deep and crisp and even on the meadows of Lazy Lee Ranch which was named more for alliterative effect than for our style of labour. Winter *was* receding, albeit too slow for our and the cows' liking. Cabin fever was advancing faster than the snow receded.

The cows, disenchanted with the quality of hay we served up on the feed-lot, had taken preemptive action and had preceded us to the stack-yard. When we arrived, we found the fence down and the haystack spread over a half acre with three hundred cows methodically stamping it into the snow. It was the last straw.

Surveying the damage done by these rebellious animals, Eldon blurted out with "Hey, let's take the day off and go to town. These ungrateful hay-burners can pull their lunch out of that mess themselves!"

"Yeah—I'll vote for that." It had been four months since we'd seen the bright lights. 'Bright lights' meant Williams Lake, population six hundred, boasting of street lights up and down Oliver Street and Railway Avenue. There was even a neon sign over Tyson's Drug Store. But it was a lot more exciting than March in a backwoods pasture.

I contemplated the excitement of playing a game of pool at Mac's Billiards, listening to the juke box at the Maple Leaf Hotel Coffee Shop, and eating a restaurant-cooked meal at the Famous Cafe. We might even catch a glimpse of one of those fair creatures rarely seen around a Cariboo swamp ranch—a girl!

However alluring the bright lights were, getting to the bright lights was another matter. The previous November we had blown all of our available assets on a 1932 Chevrolet roadster, whose main attractions were wire-spoke wheels set in the front, a rumble seat in the back, and a convertible top, which had a disconcerting habit of converting spontaneously while we were driving down the road. In addition, Andy Westwick, the previous owner, had attached a triple-throated, old-style Greyhound Bus horn under the hood.

The Department of Highways did not consider our nine-mile section of road worthy of being plowed in the winter, so "Betsy" had to be parked at the 150 Mile Garage, under the kindly eye of Jack McPhail who saw the car's ancient workings as a source of constant revenue.

With light hearts we saddled our horses and rode down the mountain, the monotony of the trip being broke at the end when a browsing moose spooked at our approach and trotted through the yard of the 150 Mile Elementary School just as the children were out for recess. The chorus of shrill screams emanating from the playground brought delighted grins to our faces.

As one might expect, Betsy, ignored for nearly four months, was not inclined to be communicative; she wouldn't start. The battery was dead and even the crank which Eldon spun vigorously failed to elicit the slightest response.

"We have ways to make you talk!" Eldon warned the reluctant roadster. Removing the spark plugs, he put a generous squirt of raw gasoline into each cylinder. The flash of a lighter held to the open head brought a satisfying "whoosh." When this was repeated twice, we screwed back the plugs, opened choke and throttle and spun the crank. Betsy came to life with a roar, announcing to all within a quarter mile that its exhaust pipe and muffler had parted company.

We tied our horses to a tree across the road from the 150 Mile Hotel, to wait our return with as much equanimity as possible. Off we went for the "metropolis", dodging pot holes and gunning the motor to race through deep, muddy ruts before we got bogged down. Finally the town of Williams Lake in all its glory came into sight.

Our first stop was the court house. We were aware that our licence plate had expired, along with both our driver's licences. That would be our first item of business, but to our surprise, the Court House door was locked and a sign told us why:

CLOSED

"Hey, how come? It's only 3:00 p.m.!" Eldon protested.

"Hmmm . . . it says, 'Open Monday to Friday.' What day is it anyhow?"

"Oh gosh—it's Saturday!" Since we worked seven days a week feeding those hungry cattle, one day was no different than another. We had forgotten that civil servants worked only five days a week.

"Oh well," Eldon shrugged, "We'll take care of all this the next time we come to town." We trooped back to our car.

"Hey! The Lees! When did you dig out of the snow?"

The cheery hail came from our friend Gordie Hyde, a 'town' friend who later became a United Church minister, posted—as I was—to the Cariboo.

"Hi Gordie—good to see you. How do you like our chariot?"

"Super." Gordie crossed the street. "Say, can I take it for a spin, I've got a driver's licence."

"Sure . . . but mind the brake. You have to shove it to the left or it catches the gas pedal on the way down."

Gordie slid behind the wheel; Eldon chose the middle, and I was left to twist the crank. Moments later we were off with a throaty roar and a shower of gravel, as Gordie let out the mustang clutch.

We turned off Oliver onto Third, dodging the quagmire in front of St. Peter's Anglican Church. Then it happened—a lady on a big bay saddle horse appeared in the centre of the street.

"Better stop—that horse looks skittish!" Eldon warned.

Gordie hit the brake; the brake hit the gas pedal. Betsy let out a terrible roar and shuddered so hard the roof converted on the spot. Confused, Gordie somehow hit the horn button adding a triple-throated trumpet blast to the din. Then the motor died.

In horrified silence we watched the big bay rear up on his hind legs, whinny with fear, and pirouette in one flowing motion before bolting down the nearest alley.

"Hey—good rider!" I exclaimed.

"Yeah—I'd be lying in the mud if it had been me!" Gordie gasped. "Here, Eldon, you'd better take over."

We made our way to the Maple Leaf Cafe and caught up on all the gossip that had happened since our last trip to town while the latest hits played on Benny Abbot's juke box in the background. Our coffee cups were refilled by an provocatively cute waitress. The time passed quickly.

"Wow, look at that clock!" Gordie exclaimed finally. "I'm late for a meeting. See you guys. Thanks for the car ride."

"Anytime!" I called after him, then, "Say, Eldon we've got time for a game of pool before supper. Let's go."

We headed for Mac's Billiards which took us past where we had parked Betsy down the block.

"Oh, oh!" Eldon came to a stop. "We've got trouble!"

Indeed we had. Two uniformed constables were showing a marked interest in our little roadster. Even as we watched, one leaned over and rubbed mud off the licence plate.

"Maybe they'll go away," I suggested hopefully.

"Are you kidding?" Eldon led the way to the offending car.

"Ah . . . good evening officers. Nice spring weather, isn't it?"

They looked at us without enthusiasm. "This your car?"

"Yep. Doesn't look like much, but it gets us there," Eldon replied, patting Betsy's rumble seat.

"Are you aware that your licence plate expired last month?"

"Well yes. But I can explain. You see it's been laid up all winter. We drove in today to get the licence renewed."

"On Saturday?"

"Well . . . um . . . we didn't realize the Motor Vehicle Branch was closed on Saturday."

The constable looked pityingly at us and moved within sniffing distance. "Let's see your driver's licence."

Eldon produced his from his wallet and handed it over. I could see we were digging ourselves into a legal black hole.

"This license expired last month, too." the constable said with grim satisfaction.

"We . . . I was going to get that renewed today as well . . . uh . . . We don't come to town very often."

The constable had his book out and was writing busily. Finally he handed us three tickets.

"Uh . . . what's the third one for?" I asked, reading them over Eldon's shoulder.

"Just what it says—driving in a manner dangerous to the public."

"Huh? What's that supposed to mean?" "We had a citizen complain. She said you were dead drunk and driving like fiends. Scared her half to death!"

A light went on—the rider whose horse had bolted! She must have galloped straight to the police station.

"You'll note you're required to be in Magistrate's Court on Friday the 17th of March at 11:00 a.m." The other constable spoke for the first time. "Oh, by the way, we'll have to impound your car."

"Impound . . . ? Hey, you can't do that!"

"Sec. 23 (1) of the Motor Vehicle Act. 'Unlicensed vehicles are subject to impoundment by the Crown'."

"But . . . but we've got to get home! Our horses are tied to a tree ten miles out!"

The constables exchanged glances. One shrugged. "All right, we'll stretch the law a bit. But get that car out of town right now and don't bring it back until it's licensed."

We drove out of town, our spirits matching the gloom of the dusk of early evening. I was thinking of the meal we'd missed and the dubious one of cold potatoes and warmed over moose parts that waited us at the ranch house.

"What a bummer!" I groaned.

"Darn it all! We didn't even get our game of pool!" Eldon complained.

"Say . . . that constable said not to bring the car back into town . . . he didn't say anything about us."

"You're right." Eldon's face lit up. "There's a road leading up into the trees . . . we could park there . . . walk back to town . . ."

We'd just placed our order in the Famous Cafe when in walked the two constables and sat down across from us. We looked at them; they looked at us. One half rose from his seat, but the other held up his hand and grinned. Nothing happened, but somehow the joy had gone out of our meal.

We played a desultory game of pool, then walked out of town, fired up Betsy and plowed our muddy way back to the 150 Mile House and our horses.

We were up early on the 17th, not at all in the light-hearted spirit of St. Patrick despite some Irish blood on grandmother's side. Luck was with us, though. We were able to hitch a ride into town and arrived only a half hour late.

In spite of the fact that Court was to start at 11:00, we counted on 'Cariboo time' and thought it prudent to first visit the Motor Vehicle Branch. Minutes later we headed for the Court, safely in possession of renewed driver's licences and a new licence plate. Our greatest concern was that we now had $23.50 between us and Magistrate Hart was known to be fond of the sentence of 'thirty dollars or thirty days'. We appeared to be the sole offenders that day, as the only occupants of the court room were the two constables and the Magistrate.

"This Magistrate's Court is now open. God save the King!" intoned one constable.

Magistrate Hart adjusted his glasses and read the first charge: Driving a 1932 Ford without a valid licence plate. "Guilty or not guilty?"

We exchanged glances. "Not guilty, your worship," Eldon replied. "We don't own a 1932 Ford . . . never have."

Magistrate Hart looked over his glasses, "Can you prove that, son?"

Eldon fished in his pocket and came up with the vehicle registration, handed it across the Bench.

"Hmmm . . . 1932 Chevrolet . . . Constable?"

"Sorry, sir . . . it was so muddy . . ."

"Hurrumph! I'd have thought, constable, that you could tell a Chevrolet from a Ford. Even I can. I'll have to throw out this charge." He picked up the second ticket.

"It says here, young man, that at the time of the complaint

you were driving without a valid driver's licence. How do you answer that?

"Not guilty, sir. I wasn't driving," Eldon answered.

"I wasn't driving, either," I added quickly.

Magistrate Hart again looked at the constables. "Your complainant made an identification, of course?" he enquired.

"Well, now that you mention it, she just said there were three wild drunks roaring around town . . ." "And the three were drunk when you questioned them?" "Well, no, they didn't appear to have been drinking . . . not these two, anyway."

"And the third?"

"Uh . . . we saw only two."

Magistrate Hart turned to us. "You boys have driver's licences now?"

"Yes sir!" We both held them out. "Case dismissed! Now, what about this dangerous driving charge?"

"I think I can explain that," Eldon said, "We turned the corner and there was this rider coming down the street . . . we didn't mean to scare her. I told Gordie to stop."

"Did you come to a *full* stop?" the magistrate asked.

"Yes sir, the driver came to a full stop."

"Well, that's all the Act requires. Case dismissed. Constable, I believe that's all for today, is it not?"

"Yes, your worship. This Court is closed. God save the King!"

Magistrate Hart gathered up his papers and left. The constables grinned and shook hands with us. "Okay, you kids, cool it, huh? Next time we just might be more accurate."

We left the court just as the noon whistle sounded, hardly daring to believe that justice had been so kind. It was time for celebration. Throwing caution to the wind, we opted for class and lunched in the luxurious Lakeview Hotel Dining Room.

How the years have rolled by. My brother and I attended universities in far cities and travelled the world, but as fate would have it, both of us ended up living in the North, I as a minister and Eldon as a medical specialist. Neither of us forgot, however, the day when the lady's horse was spooked, our apprehension of impending prosecution, and the euphoria of acquittal at High Noon in a Cow-town Court.

An Adventurous Undertaking

A visitor driving through the Cariboo today finds wide, paved highway, bustling towns and cities where residential and industrial areas show the results of effective town planning. A deeper exploration would uncover a wide variety of community support agencies, child development centres, public and mental health units, well staffed social services, Probation and Family Court counsellors, and a full range of Justice Systems.

It was not so in the turbulent 50s during the years I served in the Cariboo as a minister of the United Church of Canada. I had left eight years before to attend university and religious seminary. At that time Williams Lake was a sleepy cow-town of seven hundred people with gravel or mud streets and board sidewalks. Everyone knew everyone else. If there were a disaster, such as a house burning down or a death in the family, the community rallied around to help.

But when I returned, Williams Lake was a sprawling city of 8 000 to 10 000, depending on who was drawing the boundaries, and logging had replaced ranching as the mainstay of the economy. Four or five large planer mills dominated the area north of town called 'Smedleyville' by local residents.

Scattered around Williams Lake in a hundred-mile radius were bush mills where rough lumber was cut and trucked to the planers for refining. A cluster of rough cabins sprouted around each bush mill to house the loggers and mill-workers and their families. People came and went constantly without forming any close relationships. The friendly, personal community flavour of earlier days was gone. As might be expected, the social disorganization was horrendous. Everywhere people needed financial, physical, emotional or spiritual help.

But the support services were overwhelmed. There were two social workers, two public health nurses, and no probation services at all. The small police detachment was pushed to the breaking point. There were four churches, Roman Catholic, Anglican, Pentecostal and United. As United Church minister, I was usually called to help where the person in distress was not connected to any of the other three denominations.

The social workers, nurses and clergy tried to work as a team; and as care-givers, we attempted to meet the needs of a burgeoning population scattered from Bridge Lake to Alexandria, Horsefly to Anaheim. Each felt free to call on the others when our own resources could not meet an immediate need.

It was thus that I was called on Friday afternoon by a harried social worker. He had a problem that was beyond his mandate. Briefly he outlined his need.

A five-year-old boy had been sent to Vancouver General Hospital for treatment of a serious problem that was beyond the Williams Lake's beleaguered medical services. Sadly, the boy did not respond to treatment and died. His parents had no money to pay for his body's return to Williams Lake, and while Social Services could pay for burial in Vancouver, they had no funds to bring the body home. Did I have any ideas?

"I'll try," I responded.

My own church was struggling to survive financially; I had no charity/emergency funds on which I could draw for something like this. I canvassed the service clubs in town, but they had committed all of their funds. Finally I called my social worker friend with the only solution I could think of: I would drive to Vancouver in my battered station wagon and bring back the child's body myself.

There was a complication. I had to perform a wedding at McLeese Lake, some thirty miles north of Williams Lake, the following evening at 6:30. It was an eight-hour drive to Vancouver. I calculated my schedule carefully. If I left by 4:00 p.m. I could be in Vancouver by midnight, turn around and drive back as far as Ashcroft, then reach home in time for the wedding. It would be tight, but I could do it.

Williams Lake did not have funeral services, but one man offered services of a sort on a part time basis. At 4:00 p.m. I found Ted at the Lakeview Hotel Premises having a drink.

"I'll hit Vancouver at midnight," I said. "Can you arrange for the child's body to be ready for me at that time?"

"No problem," Ted replied confidently. "I'll phone Edwards' Funeral Home on Broadway. Everything will be taken care of."

I felt a twinge of uneasiness—perhaps because a bar was not the best setting to discuss funeral plans—but I shrugged it off. My thoughts were already on the journey ahead of me, and shortly I was heading down the highway, driving as fast as I felt I could get away with.

My calculations proved correct. At 12:10 a.m, I pulled

up in front of Edwards Funeral Home and rang the night bell. The elderly gentleman who answered my ring was kind, but regretful.

"I'm sorry, but your man in Williams Lake phoned only a half hour ago. The body is still at the hospital morgue." My heart sank, as I contemplated that closing time at the Lakeview Bar had been a mere half an hour ago; my uneasiness had been justified!

"But . . . but isn't there *anything* you can do?" I blurted.

"Not before morning. I'm here alone, you know. Oh, wait, perhaps I can be of some help." He disappeared for a minute while I fidgeted on his doorstep. When he returned he was carrying a large cardboard flower box." Perhaps the General Hospital can help you," he said without conviction. "You can use this box to hold the remains."

"But . . . but . . . !"

"Sorry, Mr. Lee. I wish we could be of more help. Good-night."

I drove to the hospital and finally found an entrance with an administrative clerk on duty. Even I thought my story was unconvincing.

"You'll have to come back in the morning," was all the clerk would concede.

"But I have a wedding in the Cariboo at 6:30 tomorrow evening!" I protested, then gave in. "What time in the morning?"

"You can come in at 7:00 a.m . . . . Someone will be here."

At 7:00 a.m. sharp I marched up to the administration desk with my cardboard box and my improbable request.

"I see . . . do you have written authorization to transport this body to Williams Lake?"

"Well, no. You see, it was all very rushed . . ."

"Um . . . will you take a seat? I'll see if Mr. Morgan is in yet."

Mr. Morgan appeared eventually and listened to me with patience, even kindness, but he shook his head. "I'd like to help, but I haven't authority to do what you ask without something on paper."

"But doesn't *anyone?* Who else can I talk to?"

"Well, the Administrator, perhaps, but he isn't here on Saturday."

"Couldn't you reach him by phone?"

"Well . . . " Mr. Morgan glanced at the clock. It was 8:30. "I guess I could call. He should be awake by now."

It must have been the sheer audacity of my request, plus a story that would be hard to invent. Perhaps it was my innocent face or apparent naivete. In any case, he gave the necessary order. I followed an orderly downstairs to the morgue where he pulled open a drawer and placed a cloth-draped object in my cardboard box.

I carried my sad burden to the parking lot and placed it in the back of the station wagon. I pondered, somewhat bitterly and sadly, as I went along, how everyone had failed this poor child that he had come to die so far from family and home.

It was 9:30 a.m. I sighed. There was three hundred and fifty miles to go on a hot August day.

It was slow going through construction zones in the Fraser Canyon. When I emerged at the other end, I was well behind schedule. North of Clinton the highway stretched straight for miles—with only a transport truck blocking my way. I started to pull out when a horn blared and a big white Chrysler shot past me, on around the truck, and was gone in a blur of speed.

I looked at my watch, breathed a fervent prayer that an understanding God would forgive my transgression, and put the gas pedal to the floor. Moments later I glanced at the rearview mirror and saw flashing red lights on a familiar blue and white car.

"Okay, Dummy," I told myself. "How are you going to explain to the Mountie how you just happen to have the body of a child in that box in the back?"

But the fates were kind. The patrolman shook his finger at me as he passed, but he was after bigger game—the Chrysler, which he overtook beyond the next hill. It was 5:00 o'clock when I pulled into Williams Lake. There was no answer at the undertaker's home. Off I drove to the Lakeview Bar.

Ted was apologetic. "Sorry about last night—it just slipped my mind."

"Okay, Ted, all's well that ends well. But, can you take over, *please?* I've got an hour to change and drive thirty miles to a wedding!"

"Oh . . . I don't have my car here, but I'll go with you to the morgue. Is 10:00 o'clock Monday morning all right for a grave-side service?"

I made the wedding with two minutes to spare.

Love's Labours Won

Charlotte was seventeen, far from home, without job or money—and four months pregnant. Ernie was twenty, had a steady job at a local bush mill, and lived in a rough cabin at the mill site. They were two young people caught up in a drama too big for them to handle alone. They needed help.

This was a scenario repeated again and again in those hectic days of the logging and lumber boom in the Cariboo. Bush mills sprang up all over the country, and because they were often remote from town, each mill spawned a cluster of shacks and cabins for the men to live near their employment.

Some brought their families to live with them, reminiscent of the early frontier days of our country. However, unlike earlier times, there was little for the children to do, and even less for their mothers. Separations were frequent and relationships formed or reformed, the players changing, the locations staying the same.

In the Cariboo of the 50s people were in a hurry, and social conventions sometimes got out of sequence. It was not unusual for the bride's bouquet to hide her pregnancy at the wedding. I quickly learned that sequence was not as important as was the attitude and commitment brought to the union. I spent long hours in counselling, when time permitted. Occasionally my first contact might be only hours before the wedding and further contact might not take place at all if the couple followed their livelihood to other parts of the province. Sometimes the man moved on leaving a wife and child and never returned to take up his responsibilities.

As United Church minister, I was often called by family friends or other care-givers in the community when there were no obvious ties to one of the other denominations. While some suggested cynically that 'the United Church would marry anyone,' I looked on each of these contacts as an opportunity to help and perhaps to offer counsel that the young couple might never receive otherwise. Some of these contacts resulted in lasting friendships. I like to think that I made a difference.

Charlotte and Ernie were different than many I had met. Although very young to consider a permanent relationship, they seemed sensible in their attitude towards life and very much in love. They both looked forward to the birth of their child. Ernie wanted only to marry as quickly as possible and make a stable life for his family. A friend who lived near the cabin Charlotte shared with her father brought them to my study. Was there something I could do?

A minister has the responsibility of ensuring that a couple have a legal right to marry before he performs a wedding service. Usually this was satisfied by the presentation of a marriage licence obtained from the local Government Agent, who also served as Marriage Commissioner. Apart from that all I could go on was what was told to me, and what I might know through other sources. I always cringed a bit when I would ask during a service—"Does any person know just reason why this man and this woman should not be united in marriage?" I resolved to be very stern should anyone ever wait until that crucial moment to come forward with an objection.

But Charlotte and Ernie did not have a marriage licence. All that they had was a crumpled form signed by Charlotte's father, giving his consent to his daughter's marriage to Ernie. Unfortunately, or fortunately, whichever way you might choose to view the matter, a 17-year-old had to have the consent of both parents. I spoke to Charlotte's father, an itinerant logger, and learned from him that he knew Ernie well and liked him. He thought that Ernie would make Charlotte a good husband. He warned me, however, that Charlotte's mother, from whom he was separated, did not like Ernie and might well object.

Mindful of a dwindling phone budget, I called Charlotte's mother in Ontario and advised her what had happened to date. Would she give consent? She would not! The phone almost sizzled in my hand as I listened to a vitriolic attack on the girl, her father, and, most of all, on Ernie. Charlotte had left home only to avoid family chores; her father was a useless drunk who had no interest in a decent marriage; her boyfriend was no man at all or he would not have gotten her pregnant in the first place. Not a chance! I hung up the phone and shook my head.

Charlotte filled me in. Yes, she had left home without her mother's permission. She was tired of babysitting the five small half brothers and sisters, while her mother was out partying; she was afraid of her mother's boyfriend who had made unwelcomed advances to her; she wanted to marry the boy who was the father of her unborn child. Since her mother had been unwilling to even consider this, she took matters into her own hands and travelled west to stay with her father, on funds that Ernie had sent.

"This may take some time," I cautioned. "Can you leave it with me for awhile . . . maybe I can work out something." I was not without resources. Being a minister in the Cariboo had quickly taught me the maxim 'the difficult can be done quickly; the impossible takes a bit longer.'

I consulted my lawyer friend, Les, who belonged to my congregation. Yes, there was a provision in the Marriage Act that allowed a county court judge to give judicial consent for a minor to marry—if it could be proved to the judge's satisfaction that withholding consent was unreasonable on the part of a parent. He warned me that such an application took time and that local County Court Judge Henry Costillou rarely gave consent when the main argument was that a girl was pregnant. He held the view that the same factors which led to an unwanted pregnancy often led to early marriage breakdown.

I could understand the Judge's reasoning. In pre-marriage counselling I had often taken the same position. Most any two kids over the age of 13 could start a baby; managing a home and family required maturity and self-discipline.

My lawyer friend agreed to prepare the legal papers necessary for a judicial review while I composed the most persuasive letter I could write to Charlotte's mother back in Ontario. There could be, perhaps, an easy way out yet if I could convince her that Ernie was behaving in a very responsible manner and was able to support her daughter.

One evening soon after this, I received an urgent call from Charlotte's friend. She related that Charlotte's father had 'moved on'—an euphemistic way of saying that he had opted out. Worse still, Charlotte had disappeared. What should be done?

I did not think it was any great mystery where Charlotte would go. With a sigh of frustration, I climbed into the clerical car and headed out into the night to find Ernie's cabin at the mill. Fortunately the mill foreman was on the site, monkey-wrenching some problem with machinery. He directed me to a cabin well back in the trees away from the road.

"I'm not sure Ernie wants visitors tonight," the foreman said, winking. "I believe he may have company already."

"Oh, I won't stay long," I replied, pretending not to understand his broad hint. I picked my way through the rubble of lumber trash, regretting that I had not brought a flashlight and finally tapped on the slab door of the cabin. There was no response. I knocked more firmly and this time heard startled voices, then the thump of feet on the floor. The door opened to a drowsy Ernie, fumbling with the belt of his trousers.

"Oh . . . Mr. Lee. Gee, what time is it, anyway?"

"About 11:00 o'clock," I replied. "Sorry to bother you at this time of the night, but I'm looking for Charlotte. Her friend said she didn't come by this evening, and she was worried. Would you have any idea where she might have gone?"

"Uh . . . well I don't . . . Oh, hell! Charlotte's here, Mr. Lee. I guess you knew that already."

"Well, yes, I sort of suspected it was the most likely place to look. Are you sure you're doing the right thing, Ernie?"

"Yes I am. I'm going to marry Charlotte one way or the other. It isn't as though we were a couple of innocent kids. We've slept together lots of times before."

I considered my position. There was something to be said

for Ernie's argument. No one was likely going to keep these two apart, and she was carrying his baby. What difference did it make if they chose to have the pleasure of each other's company when the alternatives were dubious. I was not there to return a runaway child.

While I hesitated, the defiance in Ernie's face changed to concern. "Look, Mr. Lee—Charlotte and I know you're trying to help us. If you think she should go back to town with you, well, I won't stand in the way. Only . . . only I'd really like her to stay. I want to look after her."

I made up my mind. What the heck . . . they had enough problems to work out without my adding to them. "No, Ernie, I don't think I need to disturb you anymore tonight. Just be kind to Charlotte, okay? And come in to see me when you're back in town. I care about what happens to you two."

The following afternoon I tracked down my helpful lawyer. Wasn't there any way he could speed up the process of approaching the Court?

"Hmmm . . . well, not through the usual channels," he mused. "But there's just a chance—Henry Costillou has been known to respond informally if approached in the right way. Leave it to me, I'll get back to you tonight."

I was not surprised when the phone rang that night and the lawyer came on the line. Could I round up those two kids to appear before Judge Costillou in the morning?

"But tomorrow is Saturday!" I exclaimed. "Does the Court sit on a weekend?"

"No, it doesn't, but I've talked to the Judge. He is willing to hear the application in his home at 10:00 tomorrow morning."

"Good going," I grinned into the phone. "I'll make sure Charlotte and Ernie are there."

Again I headed out the logging road in the dark, feeling equal measures of regret and embarrassment that I would have to get the young couple out of bed again. I was sure, however, that they would welcome the news that I brought. Light was beginning to show at the end of the tunnel.

I was right. Ernie came to the door at my first knock, and Charlotte appeared behind him, hastily shrugging into a robe. Ernie could borrow a car—they would be in my study at 9:30 in the morning.

"Will Judge Costillou be fierce?" Charlotte wondered anxiously.

"No, I don't think so, but he'll want to ask you some questions. Just give him straightforward answers, and don't be nervous."

Charlotte giggled. "I've never been near a Court before. I'll be shaking in my shoes."

I confess that I was apprehensive myself when we arrived next morning at Judge Costillou's lakeside home. My anxiety was quickly dispelled by the cheerfulness of the Judge's greeting. He accepted the formal papers the lawyer had prepared and perused them carefully.

"You've been in touch with the mother?" He addressed the question to me.

"Yes, sir. I've talked with her on the phone. She . . . "

"Hold on a minute," Judge Costillou held up his hand, then spoke to the lawyer. "Les . . . I think we should take Mr. Lee's evidence under oath. Did you bring a Bible?"

"No, Your Honour, I didn't think of that.

"No problem, the padre here will have one."

"I'm sorry, sir. I don't have one either."

"Now there is a workman without his tools," Judge

Costillou quipped with a grin. "Never mind, I must have one around here somewhere. Hold on a bit."

Sure enough, the Judge emerged from his den with a battered Gideon Bible in his hand. He duly swore me to tell the whole truth and I recounted all that I knew about the circumstances that brought us to his home.

Judge Costillou questioned the young people in a kind, but searching manner, and I was impressed with the thoroughness of his examination. I suspected that he was assessing attitudes more than he was looking for specific information. Finally he turned to the lawyer. "Les, may I borrow your pen?" With quick strokes he signed the Order of Consent and stamped it to register judicial approval. It was done. Charlotte and Ernie were free to marry.

The young people could scarcely contain their excitement as we drove back to town. They held hands and smiled broadly. Charlotte's eyes were shining with tears of joy.

It was a small wedding, conducted in the home of Charlotte's friend, but there were many warm wishes for their happiness and even a wedding cake. Best of all there were enough practical gifts to ensure that the young couple could set up housekeeping in style.

No one was any happier than I when I pronounced them husband and wife and paused for Ernie to kiss his bride. I was just as happy seven months later when I had the honour of baptizing their infant daughter.

Charlotte's mother had the last word in a letter which I still have in my correspondence file. "If you have so much authority with the courts," she wrote, rather wistfully, I thought, "why don't you help me get a divorce so I can marry the man *I'm* living with."

'Baby' Colleen will be thirty-four years old now. I hope

that she knows and appreciates the efforts made to ensure that she would be born in wedlock into a home made possible because, against formidable odds, love's labours won.

Sit-in At St. Andrew's

Have you heard about the time that Homer went to church? No, I suppose you have not, for our town was small, and Homer wasn't all that important. It caused a bit of local comment, to be sure, and the weekly newspaper mentioned it on the third page, but then it was forgotten. I didn't forget, however, and neither did Homer.

It happened shortly after I arrived in Williams Lake to be minister at St. Andrew's United. As is usual when a new minister takes over, there was much to be done and many people to visit. One day while I was making a pastoral call and practising the art of balancing a cup of tea on one knee and a sandwich on the other, my hostess brought up the subject.

"Mr. Lee, have you met Homer yet?"

I confessed that I had not, but added that I hoped to meet everyone before too long.

"Oh, you won't have to go looking for Homer, he'll be trying to get into the church again one of these days."

The conversation swung to another topic before I could

get my hostess to interpret this strange statement. I couldn't help thinking, however, that it would be nice to meet someone who was really *trying* to get into church.

Summer passed quickly and it was not until September that I made Homer's acquaintance. By that time I had been filled in on the story and was warned what to expect. The church's policy towards Homer was inflexible: he was not permitted to pass through its doors.

It wasn't that people didn't like Homer; oh no, not that at all. As a matter of fact almost everyone in town knew and liked Homer. He spent a lot of his time at the playground keeping an eye on things and making sure that no strange dogs approached the small children. On a sunny morning he would stroll downtown and take up his favourite position in front of the newspaper office. There he would establish himself in comfortable good humour and receive greetings from passers-by.

"Hiya, Homer, how's tricks?"

"Nice day, Homer!"

"Where have you been all week, Homer?"

Children would grin at him and even cross the street to say 'hello.' For his part, Homer would let his eyelid droop in a characteristic wink to acknowledge his popularity.

When it came to sharing in morning worship, however, it was a different matter. It was made very plain that Homer was not the least bit welcome. It wasn't that the congregations was snobbish; they wouldn't have thought that of themselves at all. It was just that one had to consider appearances. Suppose there were visitors in church? What would they say if Homer came in and sat down beside them? The matter was discussed by the church elders and dismissed with a laugh. Homer just wasn't welcome to worship with us.

I sympathized with Homer, but it wouldn't do for me to try to change things right off. Homer couldn't understand, however, and I knew he was deeply hurt. Why should he be accepted as a friend about town but be refused entry into church? Often as I greeted people coming in to worship I would see Homer across the street looking sad and sometimes bitter. No one paid any attention to him unless it appeared that he would attempt to get in; then they would tell him to be on his way.

Sometimes the children, trooping into Sunday School, would tease him, echoing their elders: "Going to church today, Homer?" they would ask, then burst into shouts of laughter. Poor Homer!

Sometimes after everyone had gone into the sanctuary I would close the outside doors and go down the steps for a sympathetic word with Homer, pat him on the shoulder, tell him I understood. I could see that Homer wasn't comforted. Off he would go up the street, every line of his departing body reflecting his hurt and rejection. I was sure that some day Homer would make good his desire to come to morning worship. And then one Sunday he did.

It was one of those warm autumn days that beckon people to hurry home from church to go for a drive in the country. The ushers had left the outside door open to allow a cool draught of air through the sanctuary. I was reading the scripture, concentrating to get just the right emphasis on the text for the day, when I became aware of a stir in the congregation. I paused in the reading to look up. There was no doubt as to the cause of the commotion: Homer was walking boldly down the centre aisle!

For a moment everyone's attention was focused on the lone figure moving determinedly towards the front. The organist swung around on her stool causing the organ to give out a shrill bleat; the ushers rose uncertainly, hesitating to interrupt the service. It appeared that Homer might make it. Then a lone church member barred his way and began to talk to him in an urgent undertone, apparently trying to get him to leave peacefully. Homer would have none of it. Having made it this far he was not going to be dissuaded by soft words.

An usher moved in to help. Sensing that they would use force, Homer showed that he knew what to do; he sat down. When they tried to lift him, he went limp and rolled over on his back.

For awhile it looked as though Homer would win, but finally he was dragged back down the aisle, his howls of protest ringing through the church. The doors closed behind him, muffling his cries, the heavy outer doors slammed shut, and all was quiet again. The ushers returned to their places, the organist turned back to her instrument, and I went on with the scripture reading.

There were no headlines. There were no demonstrations. Few people outside of our congregation even knew about the incident. I was there, however, and I can confirm the stir that was created that Sunday when Homer, the organist's basset hound, finally went to church.

To Give or to Get?

The buzzer on my desk sounded three times—my wife's signal that I was needed at the manse.

Reluctantly I laid aside the letter I was reading, my thoughts filled with disturbing news. Marriage is bliss, but why, on why, did Cupid have to sink his pesky dart into the heart of a faithful Sunday School teacher? On the way across to the manse I thought uncharitable thoughts about nomadic school teachers, especially those who stay for a year and then take a valuable church worker with them.

"This is Mr. Nordstrom," my wife introduced the man who rose as I entered the house, "he has a problem."

Mr. Nordstrom had the appearance of being genuine. He was clean shaven and neatly dressed, and he seemed frankly embarrassed to be asking for help.

"I really feel terribly foolish about this," he said wryly. "It's just that I hadn't expected to have to put so much down on that house rental. I shouldn't have done it, I suppose, but with the wife and kids arriving on the bus this weekend, I had to find a place for them to stay in a hurry."

His explanation sounded plausible. He had come to our district searching for work and had finally found a good job. Anxious to be reunited with his family, he had sent them most of his first pay cheque for bus fare. He would be paid on Tuesday. Could I possibly lend him $25 until then?

My mind was still preoccupied with he problem of finding another Sunday School teacher. Perhaps I didn't give full attention to his story. He made a good impression, however, and there was a sincere ring to his words.

"You wouldn't by any chance have experience as a Sunday School teacher?" I asked.

He chuckled, "No, but my wife has taught for years. I know she would be happy to join your staff; you couldn't keep her away."

A great load skid off my shoulders. A teacher, right out of the blue! It must be providence. "I'd be glad to lend you $25," I grinned, "We all run short once in awhile. Do you think your wife would be rested enough from her trip to start next Sunday?"

"I'm sure she would be," Mr. Nordstrom assured me, "I'll bring her over to meet you as soon as we're settled."

Mr. Nordstrom went on his way with my $25, and I went off to a meeting with two of my ministerial colleagues. The day seemed to shine a little brighter and the birds sang more sweetly.

"You look as relieved as I feel," Ed from the Temple remarked as I entered the room, "but I've got a reason to be happy. You know how badly I need a boys' leader?"

"Yes, I know. Your last one married my Sunday School teacher and took her away," I said reproachfully.

"Sorry about that," Ed grinned, "anyway, a stranger dropped by today. I discovered that he has been a boys' leader for years in a church of our denomination back on the prairies; I recruited him on the spot!" Ed chuckled. "He was in a bit of a bind, though, needed to borrow $25 to have the power turned on before his family arrives."

"I've had some good fortune, too," put in George from St. Peters, "I met a newcomer yesterday—and would you believe it? He's had experience as a choir director. I asked him if he would consider the vacancy we have and he seemed happy to agree. It's a rather odd coincidence, though; he needed $25 to get his things out of storage. I let him have it of course; choir directors don't come this way very often."

I had a sinking feeling in the pit of my stomach. "Look," I said tersely, "Was this man clean-shaven, neatly dressed, dark hair, about my build?"

"Why yes," George said, "That would be a good description of him. Did you meet him already?"

For a moment my mind raced, weighing the evidence. The conclusion I reached was not one that I liked.

"It may surprise you to know that I just gave $25 to a man who matches that description. He volunteered his wife to teach Sunday School. What did you say his name was?"

"It was Davies—Bob Davies—and yours?"

"Nordstrom, not that a name makes all that much difference in this case."

"Say, that description fits Jack Burton, the man who is going to lead our boys' group," Ed put in.

"Burton, Davies, Nordstrom—it's my guess it's the same man. Fellows, I think we've been tricked. Where did he say he was staying?"

"At Drummond Lodge," Ed and George said together.

"And that's where Mr. Nordstrom has been staying, too," I said grimly, "Brothers, let's make a pastoral call!"

The manager of Drummond Lodge looked startled at the approach of such a battery of clerics, but he greeted us pleasantly enough and asked if he could be of help.

"Nordstrom?" he thumbed through his register, "No, I don't have a guest by that name."

"How about Davies?" asked George.

"Or Burton?" interjected Ed.

"No, afraid not—no one under any of those names. What did this gentleman look like?"

Quickly we described our man.

"Why that sounds like Mr. MacDonald, the man I rented a unit to yesterday."

"Good," I said, "Could we perhaps call on Mr. MacDonald?"

"Afraid not, gentlemen, Mr. MacDonald appears to have checked out half an hour ago. He neglected to pay his bill; I've alerted the R.C.M.P."

"How about that?" Ed said glumly, as we walked away. "A phony, and he looked so genuine! We'll never see that money again!"

"Hey guys," George said soberly, "I just had a thought. You know, we're not all that much different than Mr. Davies, alias Burton and Nordstrom.

"Huh? How do you figure that?" Ed asked.

"It's like this; we were all of us out to *get* something rather than to *give* something. I guess we got what was coming to us. You know the Good Book says . . ."

"Yes, I know: 'it is more blessed to give than to receive," I agreed, "maybe you're right. We should be more interested in what our church can offer to a new family, rather than what the new family can offer to us. Let this be a lesson to us!" But it was a lesson that smarted.

Our flimflam artist was picked up by the R.C.M.P. a short time later and was discovered to have a long string of charges spread across the province. He was sentenced to six months in Oakalla. I wonder what he volunteered for there?

Cyclone Country

The phone at my bedside rang shrilly, stirring me awake. I groaned as I reached for the receiver, wondering what I would be called to do this night.

At the present time when my phone rings after midnight, it's usually one of my nine children telling me that I am a grandfather again. In those hectic days of the Cariboo in the 50s, it was usually an emergency.

At the other end of the line was a concerned night duty nurse at the Williams Lake Hospital. She reported that a baby was critically ill and might not live until morning. Could I come to the hospital and baptize the little one?

I do not now, nor did I then, believe that baptism was necessary to ensure that a baby would be welcomed by God. The Good Shepherd made it plain that little children are as close to spiritual perfection as we would come on earth: "Of such are the kingdom of Heaven." Nonetheless I accepted that infant baptism was very important to some; it was, therefore, important to me. I would go to the hospital at once.

As I entered the quiet building on the hill, I was met by the nurse who had placed the call, and was led to a crib set in the only remaining space available in the crowded hospital—the corridor.

With only thirty-two beds to serve an area of 20 000 square miles, Williams Lake's hospital was terribly inadequate to meet the need. The situation was often desperate. A new hospital building was urgently needed, but the Hospital Board, of which I was a director, was facing strong community opposition to the cost. A rancher whose opposition to the new hospital was most vocal, was himself admitted with pneumonia. I am sure he was not treated differently than anyone else, but it was perhaps ironic justice that the only place for his bed was in the hallway outside the busy administration office.

I found the baby boy in a crib covered by an oxygen tent. His little chest heaved with the exertion of drawing air into tiny labouring lungs. Clearly he was very ill.

I had never baptized a baby in an oxygen tent; the logistics temporarily baffled me. Dr. Campbell emerged from a patient's room and looked at me quizzically; then he realized my dilemma.

"Oh, I see, but don't worry. You can lift the tent. And you can use as much water as you want—it won't harm the baby." I wondered if he was telling me that nothing at this stage would be of harm, or help, to the child?

It was a simple ceremony, witnessed only by Dr. Campbell and the nurse, the latter holding my silver font. Dipping my fingers in the bowl, I drew the sign of the Cross on the baby's fevered forehead.

"David, beloved of God, I baptize you with the sign of His love. The Lord bless you and keep you."

Then, impulsively, I leaned into the crib and took a tiny hand in mine—"Hang in there, little guy! Son of Tornado, grandson of Cyclone, you come from a line of fighters. You can make it! Okay?"

✦ ✦ ✦

Cyclone Smith . . . .

The name was already a legend when I was a boy fresh arrived in the Cariboo. I think his name was Lloyd, but throughout the Cariboo he was known as Cyclone. The name came, I was told, from the way he rode the Mountain Race. This was a feature of the Williams Lake Stampede that called the best in skill and bravery from the participants and kept the watchers' hearts in their mouths. A rough track had been laid out from a point high above the Stampede Grounds, down slopes so steep a man on foot would have slipped and scrambled a torturous path, to end in the arena in front of the bleachers.

Most riders charted a zigzag path and kept their horses at a sensible rate. Not Cyclone Smith. His style was to race straight down the mountain at a speed little short of suicidal—and he always won. Thus the name 'Cyclone.' Alberta had its Pete Knight, but for the Cariboo, Cyclone Smith was its own King of the Cowboys.

As dashing as he was brave—or foolhardy—Cyclone captured the admiration of many a local lass. Riding in a Rodeo parade on his prancing black horse, Cyclone thrilled and amused the crowd by twirling his lariat and roping pretty girls along the street, one of whom was the beautiful redhead, Mary Alice Gibson. Mary was so pleased with her captor she became his friend, then his wife, and finally, the mother of his son, christened Lloyd William, but quickly nicknamed 'Tornado.'

Too restless to settle down to home and family, Cyclone drifted away from Mary. Not long after this he made the acquaintance of a woman who was hostess at a Lac La Hache guest ranch. It turned out that this was none other than an Italian princess, Beatrice Colonna Di Montechhio, who had drifted to Canada and become entranced with the ranch country of the Cariboo.

The cowboy and the Princess Beatrice became close friends and business partners in a lodge on Timothy Lake. Cyclone could not stay away from the rodeo circuit and maintained his reputation as a daredevil rider. In 1932 the story took a tragic turn. Cyclone Smith met his death as he had won his glory—in the Williams Lake Stampede. He did not die in the Mountain Race, but in a freak accident in the bucking arena when his horse fell and rolled over him. The saddle horn crushed Cyclone's chest and though his doctor used all of his skills, the damage was too massive. Cyclone died in hospital a few hours later with the Princess at his side. When the Princess learned that an old shed behind the hospital was the only place for Cyclone's body to rest until the funeral, she donated money to build a small morgue and chapel in Cyclone's memory. She directed that there should hang in the chapel a full length photograph of Cyclone holding up a coyote by the tail which some say was a live coyote. The portrait was still there when I last conducted a funeral in the chapel in the spring of 1959. The chapel is gone now, replaced when the new hospital was built in 1962. Perhaps Cyclone's picture has found a place in the Williams Lake Pioneers' Museum.

Legend has it that, as a final touch, the Princess directed that Cyclone's black horse be shot so that it might accompany him to the Great Roundup in the Sky.

Just once I foolishly signed up at the chutes to ride in the Stampede. My mount was not a bronc, but a wild range shorthorn. That cow was no lady. Not only did she pitch me unceremoniously into the dust, she clipped my head as she thundered over my hapless body. I heard bells and saw stars, and for awhile, had no interest whatever in the world around me. For me the wonders of Stampede riding would remain only a dream, and in that dream I rode with Lloyd Cyclone Smith in the forefront of a long line of legendary cowboys.

✦ ✦ ✦

This story has a happy ending after all. Little David was, indeed, a fighter. Confounding medical expectations, he rallied next day and fought his way back to health. Now married and living in the Quesnel area, David and his wife, Terry, have a son of their own named Chevy. I hope that Chevy will come to know the story of the dashing cowboy that was his great-grandfather. Perhaps he will name his own son 'Typhoon' or 'Hurricane,' that the legend may live on in the vast ranges of the Cariboo—Cyclone country.

Chilcotin Wedding

The happiest memories of my clerical years in the Cariboo were weddings among my far scattered flock. Especially memorable were those nuptial services in the ranching community. They were always a special event.

Some weddings took place in small churches that served all denominations, some in community halls, one in a granary, hurriedly swept out for the happy occasion. I remember that one well . . . it was my first wedding in the Cariboo.

It was my friend Jim Wannop who brought the request to me. Albert and Betty wanted to get married. I was happy to be part of this plan, particularly when I remembered that Betty was born when her parents lived on the hay meadows my brother and I later bought and christened, LAZY LEE RANCH.

The wedding was set for 6:30 p.m. I thought this a strange hour, since most of the rancher folk are still doing their chores at that time of day. Nevertheless I cut a meeting short and pushed the clerical Chevrolet to the limit to arrive on time.

"There's no need to hurry," Ruth Wannop assured me when I arrived at Big Lake. "Jim is giving the bride away and he's still out on the trapline."

The wedding finally got underway at 8:15, with the granary packed to the walls with family and well-wishers from all over the valley.

Consternation broke out after the wedding; somehow no one had brought anything with which to toast the bride. Not to worry, a neighbour produced a gallon of homemade potato whisky, and the bride was duly honoured. In fact, when I stopped in a Beaver Valley a few days later, the bride was still being toasted!

Big Creek . . . .

Big Creek was a small ranching community in the highlands of the Chilcotin, some eighty-five miles west of Williams Lake. I did not go to Big Creek often, partly because my clerical responsibilities took me to dozens of other communities, partly because Rev. George Fielder of the Cariboo Anglican diocese agreed to go West if I went East and South. On months that had five Sundays, however, I headed for Big Creek where my welcome was always warm.

Although not of my denomination, the Church family took their religious commitment seriously. I was honoured when they asked me to conduct the marriage ceremony for their son and his bride. I looked forward to this trip into the deep Chilcotin.

Previous experience with Chilcotin roads in breakup time had made a lasting impression on me. Some swampy sections were so notorious, they were given permanent names. The very sight was enough to daunt the uninitiated. Often broken poles and splintered planks, floating in water-filled ruts, gave evidence of desperate measures some motorist had taken to free himself from the bogs. Usually, a vehicle so mired could be extricated only with a tractor or a team of horses from the nearest ranch, however ingenious the hapless driver might be.

Giving caution preeminence, I headed west across the Fraser River, well equipped with shovel, tire chains, and a coil of rope long enough, I hoped, to reach a tree and form a Spanish windlass should I become hopelessly bogged. And I allowed myself a full four hours to travel eighty-five miles to the Church ranch. There were some places where all I could do was slam the gears into low, tramp on the gas pedal and pray. I like to think that the Almighty cloaked the underside of the car with an unbreakable shield to protect its tender vitals.

Four hours later I drove under the pole gateway of the Ranch and heaved a sigh of relief. Let the festivities begin.

The Church home was filled to bursting for the wedding, and many and warm were the wishes for happiness to the bride and groom. After the ceremony everyone joined in a wedding feast such as only Chilcotin hospitality could assemble.

Johnny and Bonnie were anxious to get away as they planned to reach Kamloops for their honeymoon night. They were mindful of the state of that eighty-five miles of Chilcotin highway before they reached pavement at Williams Lake. No one had noticed the temporary absence of several ranch personnel while dinner was in progress.

Finally everyone gathered in the muddy yard as the happy pair loaded their bags. "Goodbye! Goodbye!" chorused the crowd. Johnny turned the key, the starter ground fruitlessly. The motor would not start.

"I'll get the tractor—give you a pull," someone shouted.

Round and round the feed-lot the puzzled groom was pulled. Every time they came by the house the well-wishers shouted another chorus of "Goodbye!"

Finally Johnny smelled a rat. He lifted the hood of his car and very quickly discovered that the rotor had been removed from the ignition. Mysteriously, someone just happened to know where a rotor could be found. To a final chorus of farewells, the young couple were on their way.

The first ranch gate was roped tightly with loop after loop of rope—Johnny's special lariat. Approaching it with exasperation, Johnny noticed a very pungent odour—someone had smeared the rope liberally with Limburger Cheese. Wincing at the loss of his lariat, Johnny chopped the gate free with an axe. Well, at last they were on their way!

Relief was short-lived. A half mile down the road they were stopped again—this time by a tree fallen across the road. It was freshly cut! The axe turned out to be the dullest one on the ranch. It took twenty minutes of hard chopping to removed the obstacle. Muddy and dispirited, Johnny stowed the axe and started the car. A half mile further they came to another tree. Someone had gone down the road with a chain saw and methodically dropped a tree wherever there was no hope of going around it.

When I caught up to the wedding party two hours later, Johnny, soaked and muddy from head to foot, had his car jacked up and was desperately trying to free something from underneath. Wired tightly to the frame was the coyote-chewed remains of a yearling steer's carcass.

Yes, the wedding couple finally reached Williams Lake, where they stopped at a local garage to remove cans, bones and other detritus so carefully attached by hands unknown. Johnny could still manage a grin. "Just wait," he said.

"There's another wedding coming up."

There was indeed. John Siebert, cattle foreman at the ranch, married Rosalie Church. Because the wedding was on Sunday and I had a worship service to conduct in Williams Lake, the Church family chartered a float plane to fly me to a lake near the ranch.

Johnny had a strong suspicion that Siebert had orchestrated the misfortunes that befell him on his wedding day, and plotted his revenge. The Siebert car was given most elaborate attention with innovations that would make revenge sweet and complete.

When the wedding reception was over, the happy couple said their goodbyes, then were whisked away to a nearby ranch. To the dismay of the collaborators in revenge, the bride and groom departed on saddle horses for a honeymoon in the alpine meadows of the Big Creek Range.

Yes, ranching community weddings were special events, and Chilcotin weddings were the best.

He Saw With Other Eyes

When the manse phone rang it was usually a call for action on my part, whether within the boundaries of Williams Lake, or in some corner of my widespread charge fifty or a hundred miles away. In those frantic days of the 50 s, there were few calls that were routine.

This time the call had been for me, personally, a sad call from home; Grandpa was gone. A chapter in my life was closed. As I turned away from the phone, a host of memories flooded my consciousness. How much his life had shaped mine, from early childhood to the university years, to the achievement of my chosen career. A picture formed in my mind—Grandpa standing tall and straight, his horn-rimmed glasses in his hand. Like a newsreel in reverse the years rolled back to the Cariboo ranch where I had spent my boyhood years:

✦ ✦ ✦

"The hay is ready to cut isn't it, Grandpa?" I shuffled my feet impatiently.

We stood at the edge of the meadow watching the wind blow ripples across the waving grass, a boy whose curly blond head failed by inches to reach the other's shoulders, and a man whose wrinkled face and greying hair marked the passing of many years.

"Shall I get the horses?" I pressed on for an answer. This was an important year for me—I had graduated from the hay fork; for the first time I would be permitted to drive a team of horses and operate a mowing machine. I could hardly wait.

But Grandpa was not to be hurried. He had crumbled the full heads of timothy in his hand, sniffed and tasted them as farmers have done for centuries to determine if the grass were ripe enough to cure properly. Now he stood in deep reflection, his glasses clutched in one calloused hand, his eyes roving over the hayfield and beyond to the hills blurred in summer haze, and above them to the blue sky in which a few puffs of clouds floated like dumplings in a stew.

I knew that my Grandpa was sensing and evaluating all the factors that would give him a clue to what the weather would do in the next few days: the direction of the wind, the shape of the clouds, the density of the haze.

"It looks all clear ahead!" Grandpa said finally. "You can hitch up your team to the mower." He put his glasses back on and I raced to the barn, whooping with excitement.

Grandpa always took his glasses off and held them in his hand when he wrestled with some problem. "I can see better that way," he would say. And he could, I'm sure; not those things that were right there in front of him—he had trouble reading the fine print of the family Bible—but the things that were not visible to just anyone and had to be grasped by other senses. Like the weather.

I remember watching Grandpa standing that way, glasses in hand, when he looked over the smouldering ashes of what had been our home. Nothing had been saved from the disastrous fire. My brother and I had been the only ones at home on the ranch when the fire had broken out and we had fought a losing battle with the flames. Now we stood by fearfully, wondering what Grandpa would do.

Those had been Depression years and the simple task of keeping the family fed and clothed was one that meant a continual struggle. There was no money to rebuild the home or to buy furniture. How could it be done?

I'm sure that the clouds that hid the future that day must have been heavy and dark. But Grandpa had something better than glasses—he had a deep faith that no obstacle would be too great to overcome.

"We'll build a log house," he said, straightening his shoulders. "There are logs for the cutting in the woods." A few months later a new home rose from the ashes of the old and somehow the money to furnish it was found.

Although I was too young to remember, I'm sure that Grandpa must have stood the same way, glasses in hand, when he made the decision to take his family from a pleasant farm in California to a wilderness ranch in the Cariboo, far north of the Canadian border. How else could he have seen that this move would be the best for his family, would give them a place to live, a place to grow when the Depression years took the jobs away from so many small farmers in the South?

There were many years of hard work ahead, but hard work can build character. My brother and I would grow strong and sturdy riding horses, sawing wood, or driving the haying equipment. We learned to put everything we had into the task at hand, and to be proud of our accomplishments. Work habits that we learned from Grandpa would benefit us in whatever employment we found in later years. Yes, we sometimes groaned at the hours we were expected to put in, and grumbled that there was not enough time for play. Somehow it was usually about the time that Grandpa would declare a holiday and take us all for a day of fishing.

Gruff in manner, Grandpa seemed to have difficulty showing affection. As a small boy I sometimes wondered if I were important to him, or if I were only one of the responsibilities that he had taken on. One winter day I was with Grandpa while he was unloading hay from the sleigh to the roof of the cattle shed. A lively nine- year-old, I was amusing myself by burrowing through the fragrant hay, making a tunnel to my own private hiding place. Unfortunately I tunnelled out into space and landed on my back on the frozen ground eight feet below. All the lights went out. When I opened my eyes I found myself cradled in Grandpa's arms as he strode across the barnyard towards the house—and behind those horn-rimmed glasses there was the glint of tears. I had my answer: Grandpa cared!

I remember another time when in my late teens I was feeling overworked and under-appreciated. Grandpa had ridden off in the morning to go to Williams Lake for the day, and I was left with the hard, boring job of splitting fence rails. Yes, I knew that Abraham Lincoln split rails on his way to becoming president of the United States, but I could see no such glorious result from my labours. My mind seethed with resentment. When Grandpa returned home, to my amazement, he produced for me the most beautiful pair of leather chaps I had ever seen. They had surely cost more than he could possibly afford; it was a gift that cleared my eyes to see how wrong I had been when I thought my work was unappreciated.

I remember the proud look on Grandpa's face when I graduated from university at the head of my class. When I took my vows of ordination, he put his hand on my shoulder and in a husky voice told me that God had put his seal on me and my life could never be the same. It wouldn't be.

Grandpa lived on past his eightieth year, accepting each year of life as though it were a gift from God to be enjoyed to the fullest. His children were married and established in homes of their own. There were grandchildren who brought great-grandchildren for him to admire. Each one was a delight to him and he seemed to draw a never-failing satisfaction from seeing his own values being projected into the future through his descendants. For him responsibilities were past; now there was only one great challenge to be faced.

And then the call came. Grandpa was gone. Active to the end, he was out in the pasture searching for his cattle when the last call came. They found him there, lying in the grass—with his glasses clutched in his hand.

Had Grandpa been able to see beyond this last barrier to the good things prepared by God for those who love Him? Had he been able to use his eyes of understanding to know that here, too, all was clear ahead?

A few days later I was sure that this had been so, for among the papers in his safety deposit box was a note he had left for us to find. In his firm, confident scrawl he had written: "Goodbye, kids, I'll see you all again."

Lady of the Lakes

There were times in my Cariboo ministry when crisis followed hard upon crisis. Tragedy and sudden death were common in this time of lumbering boom and its resulting social disorganization. Even joyful times such as weddings and baptisms took their toll on my store of energy. I found that I had to make time to recharge my emotional batteries.

Sometimes we loaded the children into the clerical car and drove off to explore some forestry road far from jangling phones or ringing doorbells. Sometimes we took the Likely road and spent a quiet day with rancher friends at Big Lake, or rented a cabin for an overnight stay at some remote resort. Occasionally I needed a day just to myself, and I was grateful that my family understood and made it possible.

My favorite place for solitary recharging was the Knife Creek Range where I had spent my boyhood. There I walked old trails and relived the times when my brother and I had roamed the woods during carefree summer days. It was here that I came in late afternoon one September day.

The road that led from the 141 Mile House to Squawks

Lake was not one that invited fainthearted travellers. The mudholes were deep and the rocks were high and sharp. It didn't stop me, however; I knew the location of all the hazardous spots. Parking my car below the lakes, I wandered along a trail above Knife Creek until I came to a beaver dam. Eldon and I had fished and swum here as boys and later set mink and muskrat traps in season. I sat down on a fallen tree trunk and opened memory lane. And then I remembered her—Old Annie—Old Annie Basil. In moments the passage of 20 years was erased and I was a ten-year-old, eager to learn about the world around me.

✦ ✦ ✦

Annie came, I recall, with the regularity of the seasons, year after year.

It might be in that interlude of early spring when winter had given up its harsh grip and nature worked its miracle of renewal. It might be when summer haze lay heavy on forested slopes and sunbeams filtered through the pines of the blueberry swamp to ripen plump fruit for the delight of bird, beast and man. It might be during the first crisp days of Indian summer when gold and scarlet from poplar and sumac joined in the task of laying a rich carpet on the forest floor; when fat young partridges dusted along the roadsides, and proud antlered bucks roamed the alder thickets.

At one of these special times she would come, hobbling along the road, one dusky hand holding a gnarled walking stick and the other grasping the lead-rope that made her one with the ancient grey nag that carried her camping equipment.

We called her Old Annie—everyone did, and though she

bore the surname of Basil I never heard that name used. Annie was her Christian name and old she certainly was, how old no one seemed to know. "When Annie was a little girl, white men came to this country," she told us, her eyes twinkling as she worked away at a basket in front of her camp. My brother and I never tired of listening to her stories or of watching her hands which always seemed to be busy. The tales she told us did much to recreate in our minds a picture of the glorious past of her people.

Although Old Annie was a very sociable person and loved to sit and visit by the hour, she was also a solitary wanderer who travelled alone with no other company than her faithful packhorse. When she tied her horse to our gate post and stopped for a visit, we put up a tent for her and urged her to stay. She always stayed, a few days or a week—time worried her not. She had about her an atmosphere of timelessness that gave a quiet rebuke to the hurry and bustle of the world about her. One morning she would be gone, moving back into the wilderness to find the solitude of nature that gave her delight and peace.

Sometimes Eldon and I found her sitting motionless beside a beaver pond, a fishline dangling from the end of a long pine pole, patience and contentment written in every line of her face. Intent on her fishing, she wasn't interested in idle chatter, but would always nod and smile. We would go on about our business with no thought of disturbing her.

Sometimes we would find Annie's campsites after she had gone. They were left ready for her return, a small supply of dry wood piled near the neat circle of stones, and usually the polished sticks with which she kindled her fire.

Old Annie seemed as much a creature of the past as of the present. She could discuss current events with intelligence and wit, and she loved to talk about the daily life of the Reserve and to share humorous incidents from the lives of those around her. When on the Reserve she was faithful in attending the Mission Church and dressed to suit the occasion, a far cry from the ragged clothes that were a part of her nomadic wanderings. From Red Cross nurses she had learned the skills of a practical nurse and midwife and had brought into the world some prominent citizens, now reaching senior-citizen status themselves.

More true to Annie's image, however, was the quiet figure relaxed by her tent, hands busy with basket and bead work, but thoughts a half century or more in the past as she spun a web of adventure for two small boys who hung on every word. And what stories they were . . . Hardships and danger, Indian wars and buried gold . . . Each tale seemed to bear its own stamp of authenticity and in the telling Annie appeared scarcely conscious of the present, but living again in days long gone by.

Old Annie spoke the dialect of her people fluently, we knew, but with us she always used English in the soft, drawling sing-song inflection of her race. There were two exceptions to this: for things that particularly pleased her, she would use the Salish adjective "Hie-yu," nodding her head vigorously and otherwise showing every evidence of pleasure. On the other hand, for something that displeased her, she would use the explosive "Hai-lo!" following it with disapproving clicks of her tongue.

Sometimes Annie would take us into the woods to share with us her vast store of woodlore. On one such trip she paused by a clump of wild lily plants, then, using a sharp stick, she probed in the ground. Presently she produced several small bulbs which she handed to us to taste.

"Hie-yu, good," she exclaimed, smacking her lips, then grinned broadly at the wry expressions on our faces as we spat out the bitter root. "You cook him," she explained, "then he just like a potato."

Another time Annie showed us a bush laden with bright red berries. She picked a handful and squeezed the juice into her mouth, inviting us to do the same. Again we were amazed at the horrible soapy taste of the fruit. Annie laughed openly at our discomfort. "You have to learn to like him—Indian boys think hooshem berry juice just like soda pop!"

Perhaps the most fascinating of Old Annie's activities was her skill in making birch-bark baskets. Starting with a piece of unblemished bark, she would carve and fold until she had fashioned it into a square vessel with slightly rounded corners. Next she prepared thongs, not of thread or sinews, but of long fibers stripped from a length of green spruce root. Some of these she dyed scarlet with the juice of hooshem berries, others a bright blue from huckleberries. Black came from the coals of her campfire and yellow from the golden plumes of the dandelion or snapdragon. With the point of her skinning knife serving as an awl, she made rows of tiny perforations along the edge of each seam, then her fingers fairly flew as she wove the multi-colored roots in and out, in and out, until there was a bright border up each corner and completely around the top. The finished product was surprisingly attractive and useful basket. I still have one of them on display.

There came a spring when we waited in vain for Annie to make her usual visit. Later we learned that her relatives, afraid that something might happen to her in the bush, would not let her go away again on her own.

Annie was not to be so easily dissuaded; when the blueberry season arrived, Annie arrived also. She moved more slowly, it is true, but then her old packhorse had reached the age when he was not difficult to pace.

"I run away!" Annie reported gleefully. "Andrew think he keep me home but I fool him. I tell him, 'Annie just go down to the store at the 150 Mile' . . . then I go quick down the road." She chuckled with delight, hugely enjoying the thought of how she had outwitted her guardians.

Annie did not go to the Lakes, however, but was content to accept the hospitality of our tent and spend the days near our ranch. Most of the time she sat in the sun by her camp, content to listen to our small-boy chatter. When she readied her pack to return to the Reserve she was reluctant to leave, turning again and again to repeat her goodbyes. It was as though she could sense that she would never come that way again. Finally she walked away, the old horse hobbling along behind her, the two of them tired emissaries from another day.

I saw Old Annie once more the following spring when we made an infrequent trip to the Reserve. She was sitting in front of her tiny log cabin, seemingly watching the goings and comings of her neighbors, but in reality almost blind. Her shrunken figure was wrapped in successive layers of sweaters and shawls. At my greeting a smile of recognition flitted across her face, but when she spoke her face took on the passiveness of resignation.

"I go no more to the Lakes," she said sadly. "My old horse, he is dead. Now Annie die, too."

Old Annie lived on, however, for several more years. I went away to university in Seattle and for a time lost track of familiar people and places. One day I read an item from the hometown newspaper describing a fire on the Reserve. An elderly woman had perished in the blaze. Even before I read the name, I sensed that it was my boyhood friend, Old Annie Basil.

✦ ✦ ✦

My thoughts were broken by the swish of wings as a covy of ducks swooped in to a landing on the beaver pond. With a start I came back to the present, but the memories persisted. How much my life had changed in 20 years! There were the university years, marriage and a young family, my return to the Cariboo as a minister; but how little had changed here. A few feet from where I stood the grass grew up through a circle of stones where once there had been a campfire. I was certain that it was one that Annie had left long ago, tidy and ready for her return.

Twilight came and with its coming the beaver came out to trace silvery paths on the surface of the pond. A trout leaped high to catch a drifting fly and landed with a plop and a dash of spray. High overhead a nighthawk chirped in its circling flight. I could almost see Annie there, her face a picture of contentment as she surveyed *her* fishing grounds. Was it only imagination conjured by the heady scents of the summer evening? Or was it Old Annie's voice echoing softly through the shadowy pines in praise of God's creation: "Hie-yu, good!"

A Man of Influence

"Intolerance!"

Down went a tall burdock stalk to be added to the growing heap by the back walk.

"Intemperance!" Another stalk fell beneath my invincible sickle.

"Racism! Anger! Self Righteousness! Meanness!" Each fell without mercy and left the walk better for its fall.

Perhaps a minister can be permitted his moments of eccentricity—if it's Monday afternoon. We returned from a holiday to find that weeds had all but taken over the yard. Now I was up to my waist in the last stronghold, a stand of stout burdocks along the back walk. To bring an element of challenge to the chore I gave each stalk the label of one of humankind's shortcomings then dispatched the scapegoat with a ruthless swing of my sickle.

"Deceit!"

"I beg your pardon?"

Slowly I straightened up, favouring my tired back, then turned towards the voice. A young man stood at the gate, hand on the latch. Seeing the puzzled look on his face I chuckled.

"Don't mind me," I volunteered. "Just talking to myself. What can I do for you?"

"Am I speaking to Mr. Lee?" I nodded.

"Well, I am pleased to meet you; your neighbours certainly hold you in high regard!" He advanced through the gate and held out his hand. "I'm Don Appleman."

I searched my mind: Church Office? Bible Society? Youth Services? The name rang no bell. I'd just have to play it by ear. "You're not from Williams Lake?" I asked.

"No. I'm representing a well-known publisher in the field of Research Education."

"Oh. . . . " a glimmer of light dawned. "You're selling encyclopaedias."

A distinctly pained expression crossed his face before he answered.

"Oh no! I'm doing an advance survey for our research department."

"Well," I answered. "That's good news. I was about to tell you that I'm not in the market for any books right now. What brings you to my door?"

"My publisher is interested in placing a set of our latest research work with one or two people of influence in each community—as a gift, of course—so that they can evaluate the effectiveness of the material. Your neighbours seem to think that your are the most influential person around here."

"Umm . . ." I hesitated, still suspicious. "And in return . . . ?"

"Why we wouldn't expect anything in return, except a letter from you giving your honest opinion of the set. Of course we are convinced that you will be delighted with the material, but that's entirely up to you."

"And you're sure you are not selling books?"

"Mr. Lee, do I look like the sort of person who would go around deceiving people?"

I took a moment to hold inventory: neat, conservative cut suit, bright but not bold tie, new briefcase; yes, he did look like a book salesman, and, heaven knows what 'deceivers' I'd found book salesmen to be over the years.

"Well, we may as well go in the house and discuss this in comfort." I led the way around the walk and met my wife at the flower beds. She straightened up as we approached, her eyes taking in the briefcase.

"No books." she said firmly.

"Mr. Appleman isn't a book salesman, dear," I said reassuringly. "He wants to give us a set of encyclopaedia."

"For how much?"

Mr. Appleman chuckled good naturedly. "I can see that Mrs. Lee has had dealings with book salesmen before. Some of them are a shifty lot." He grinned. "I've just been explaining to your husband that we are looking for several knowledgeable people who can evaluate our new set of Research Volumes. No obligation at all."

"Oh, well, I have to round up the youngsters. You go ahead. Remember though . . ." she admonished as I walked past, ". . . nothing in the book budget!"

Mr. Appleman seated himself and extracted from his bulging briefcase a large volume suitably encased in scarlet binding, opened it up and caressed its pages. "This is really an executive type binding we're giving you," he announced. "Most of the sets issued for general sale will have a much plainer binding."

"I'm still not clear just why you are going to give me a set, absolutely free." I emphasized the 'free' just to make sure.

"Quite frankly, Mr. Lee, we may be taking something of a gamble. But we're counting on the fact that in Williams Lake, as in other towns, people take their cues from those they respect and admire. I'm confident that a person whom others consider as influential as yourself will justify our investment in giving you a free set."

Almost unconsciously I squared my shoulders and sat a bit straighter—as befits a man of influence. It was nice to know that I was held in that high regard, even though Sunday congregations were certainly nothing to boast about!

"Well, that's kind of you to have such confidence in my position," I began. "though I can't say that I agree with you entirely. Are you leaving the set now?"

"Oh no. The books are not off the press yet. Your set should arrive in three or four weeks." He pulled some official looking papers from his briefcase. They looked like contract forms to me and I said as much.

"Well, ah . . . I suppose you might call them that," he admitted, chuckling. "Actually, I suppose I should make a confession. The set is absolutely free, just as I promised. However, my publisher wants to be sure that your set is always up to date—this is one of its strong points—so they are asking that each person who accepts a free set agrees to purchase the Year Book for ten years. This will be an extremely useful volume and well worth the nominal charge . . . "

" . . . of how much?"

"Only $24.95, really only *pennies* a day," he said quickly.

"Well . . . " I hedged, thinking of the depleted budget. "I suppose I *could* manage $24.95 a year."

"Well, uh, there's one other provision. The publisher

would like you to pay for the ten Year Books in advance; of course you can spread the payments out over a year, or longer if you wish."

"Oh . . . " the bait was beginning to show the hook. "Well, in that case. . . . " I picked up the volume he had placed temptingly on the table in front of me. It *was* an attractive book, smooth glossy pages, full colour illustrations, good print. "Look, this is a slightly different proposition. I'll have to discuss it with my wife. If you will pardon me for a few minutes.

"By all means." Mr. Appleman's expression belied the readiness of his answer. "Remember," he called as I headed for the kitchen, " . . . the set itself doesn't cost you a penny."

My wife looked doubtful when I outlined the proposal. "I suppose we could use an up to date set," she conceded, "but that's a lot of money."

"Hmmm. I suppose you are right . . . but I could refrain from buying any other books for the next year or so . . ."

"Ah, but you know your weakness!"

I ignored this barb. I suppose I did have a few, well, perhaps forty or fifty books that served no more useful purpose than to set off to advantage those Christmas book-ends. "It's only the Year Books we're paying for. . . . "

"Oh I guess we can manage it. . . . " reluctantly. We returned to the living room.

"Now, if you will just sign this contract here, and here . . . ."

"Just a moment," my wife put in. "What are those coupons for?"

"That's how you get your Year Book. Each year you clip off one of these coupons and send it in, together with $6.50 . . . ."

"$6.50! I thought the contract covered the cost of the Year Books."

Mr. Appleman began to look uncomfortable. "That's only a charge for Research Service. Just send in any question you want answered . . . and of course there are shipping charges, change of address servic . . . it's really less than forty cents a month."

"These 'pennies a day' grow into dollars. By the way, I'd like to see one of these Year Books. Have you one in your briefcase?"

"Why certainly, only a sample type, of course." He groped in the case and produced a less promising binder. "You'll note that it comes in four parts—that way your set is never more than three months old. Why don't you look through that while your husband finishes signing the contract," he suggested hopefully, and again arranged the papers, handing me a pen.

"Wait, stop the press!" my wife exclaimed. "It says here that this is a Quarterly Review—with an annual subscription price of $6.50." She fixed an accusing glare on the now squirming salesman. "The $6.50 really pays for the Year Book, and the ten instalments of $24.95 pay for the encyclopaedia! Free—ha! What were you saying about shifty salesmen?"

Mr. Appleman stuffed his books and unsigned contract back into the new briefcase and made a rather disgruntled departure.

"Well, Mr. Influential Citizen, are you going to get those weeds down before supper?" my wife asked, rudely jarring me from a brief reverie on the fallibility of man.

In the back yard I advanced on the largest remaining burdock, clothing it as I approached with a conservative suit and tie, a new briefcase . . . But wait, who was really at fault? Honesty forced me to change perspective.

"Conceit!" I christened the stalk, just before the sickle's swing, and sheepishly added it to the pile.

A Meaningful Encounter

I was late in finishing my rounds at the local hospital. When I slipped into our favourite booth at the Coffee Shop, my two colleagues were well into their first cups and engaged in heated debate.

"What's the subject today?" I enquired.

"We are trying to establish a definition of what constitutes a pastoral call," said the Rev. Ed. "I maintain that a pastoral call is any contact with a family that involves a meaningful encounter."

"On the contrary," interposed George from St. Peter's. "It's my contention that a pastoral call must be a *planned* visit for a specific purpose!" He stirred his coffee vigorously to emphasize the point.

"I'm sure you will . . . " they both began at one time, then stopped, confused.

"You're *both* sure I will agree—is that what you were about to say?" I put in, amused.

"Well . . . " Ed commented sheepishly, "Suppose you tell us what *you* think."

"Hmmm . . ." I gave the matter some time to percolate

before replying. "The phrase is capable of several definitions. If one is thinking in terms of a congregational report, then perhaps George has the answer. On the other hand, if one is thinking of a significant contact by a minister with one of the community, well . . . Let me tell you about a *call* I made last week."

I was on my way home from a visit up river at Soda Creek when I decided on the spur of the moment to investigate one of the clusters of homes growing up around a new planer mill. A young mother answered my knock at her door.

"Good afternoon," I began. "I'm the minister from St. Andrew's United Church. I thought I would stop by and see if . . . " At that moment two things happened: the lady of the house smiled and said, "Won't you come in, please," and somewhere from behind her there came a great howl of pain. I stepped in; the mother flew to the kitchen.

"John-ee! What have you done to yourself?"

Johnny had obviously cut his finger severely. Blood was pouring out of his clenched hands and leaving a trail across the floor, and all the time Johnny roared with pain and fright.

"Oh my goodness!" cried my hostess. The cut *was* an impressive one and showed that a new jackknife had received its initiation in blood. "I get so upset at the sight of blood—I'm going to take him over to Barbara next door, she's a nurse. Will you excuse me, please?"

At that moment a smaller edition of the injured boy came out of another room, rubbing sleep from his eyes. Mother looked at him in dismay. "Oh Ricky, you weren't supposed to be up yet—whatever will I do with you . . . !" But Ricky showed no inclination to return to his interrupted nap.

All this time I had been standing inside the door, somewhat nonplused over this sudden turn of events. "Look," I volunteered, "I'm pretty used to youngsters; have three back in the manse. If Ricky will let me, I'll stay with him while you go have Johnny's hand patched up."

"Oh, I couldn't . . . " she began, flustered. Johnny roared even louder. "Well . . . if you wouldn't mind? I'll be only a few minutes."

"Right-o, you run along . . . we'll manage, won't we Ricky?" Finger in mouth, younger brother grinned his approval, and away went Johnny and his mother for first aid.

I scooped up Ricky to show my good intentions and immediately became aware that all was not well. "Look, Ricky," I ventured conversationally. "Do you know where your mother keeps your dry pants?"

"Panss?" Ricky wriggled to the floor and scooted off to the room from which he had first emerged. In a moment there was a crash and a wail of distress. Sure enough, he had found a pair of dry pants, but had also pulled a dresser drawer down on top of his head.

The changing operation was making good progress when there was a knock at the door. Thinking that Johnny's mother had probably locked herself out, I went to the door with the bare and wriggling Ricky under my arm. To my surprise there was a man with a briefcase standing on the porch. He looked startled.

"Yes?" I asked, somewhat impatiently, I suppose.

"Pardon me," he recovered his poise. "I'm a visiting Bible student and I stopped by to discuss . . . "

I permitted myself an inward chuckle and succumbed to temptation. "Good of you to call, but we're not interested."

"Perhaps your wife . . . " he suggested, holding his ground.

"Sorry, my wife doesn't live here."

"But . . . but the lady I talked to last week . . . . " he looked genuinely puzzled.

"Oh," I laughed. "That wasn't my wife!"

His eyes took in the squirming Ricky, the clothesline full of children's clothes. "But . . . . "

"Sorry, I really have to leave you," I concluded pleasantly, and closed the door. Through the window I could see him stop at the gate, shake his head and write something in his note book.

"Ricky," I grinned. "You and I have just won a victory!"

Ricky grinned back as though he shared in the conspiracy. Suddenly from the kitchen there came a great spitting and sputtering. I rushed out to find a full canner of jars boiling over onto the stove and floor. "Hey!" I called to the boy. "Stay out of that water—*hot!*"

Gingerly I lifted the lid from the kettle and closed the damper on the stove. The water ceased its angry rolling. While I was doing this, the telephone rang; there was a patter of small feet: "He-row?"

I retrieved the receiver from Ricky and added redundantly. "Hello?"

"Bill . . . ?" came a voice hesitantly.

"I'm afraid Bill isn't here," I answered. "Is there a message?"

"But I thought . . . uh, who . . . ? Oh, never mind, I'll call later." The line went dead.

"I hope *Bill* is your daddy," I said to Ricky. "Whoever that was must be wondering what's going on." The kettle boiled over again. I repeated the previous tactics and returned to the front room to find my young charge eying me owlishly.

"Not again . . . !" I exclaimed. "Okay, sport—find me

some more dry pants." At that point, to my frank relief, Ricky's mother appeared at the door.

"I'm terribly sorry to have been so long. Barbara thinks Johnny should have a couple of stitches to close that cut. She's going to drive us in to the doctor. Thank you so much! Which church did you say you were from?"

"St. Andrew's United, corner of Third and Cameron," I answered. "We would be happy to have you and your family worship with us if you don't already have a church home."

"Thank you. You've been a big help today. Please call again—I promise not to make you baby-sit next time." And then she was off and I climbed into my car and continued homeward.

"You see," said Ed, "your story proves my point. It was a *meaningful encounter.*"

"Ah, but did you carry out your *purpose* for going there in the first place?" countered George.

"Well, we had a new family at church last Sunday," I answered. "And Ricky gave me a big grin at the door."

Parable of a Rutted Road

It was one of those rare days when nature seemed most disposed to smile. Golden-hued leaves from cottonwood and birch drifted down and left a royal carpet scarcely disturbed by the passing of car wheels. Haze hung low on the hills and silver spider threads floated lazily over fields where cattle grazed.

I was out exploring one of the more distant parts of the Williams Lake Charge and, as usual, had stopped at one of the first houses in the district to ask directions to the ranches strung out along the valley floor. My informant was most helpful and even drew a map to show who lived where and which of the numerous side roads led to homes. Her pencil paused after she had drawn in one short road.

"There's only old Mr. M—— living up there," she explained. "He isn't interested in the church. In fact he doesn't like ministers at all. You won't need to waste your time going in to his place."

In due course I came to the point where this road wound off through the trees, little more than a rutted trail that bore witness to the fact that Mr. M. had very few visitors. I had some doubt that I could even navigate the road without risking damage to the vulnerable undercarriage of my clerical car. Seizing on this practical thought, I went on towards the next ranch where I had been promised a warm welcome.

For some reason, however, as I drove along something was bothering me, nibbling at the edge of conscience; and then I remembered. I thought of another year and another road . . . and therein lies a story which I will call "The Parable of a Rutted Road."

The highway which formed the only link between the sparsely settled Interior and the Coast was not a royal road in those times, but a dusty stretch of washboard, ruts and chuckholes. No one drove fast for obvious reasons but it was still easy to miss the break in the forest where a little side road declared its independence and wound off into the trees.

It was not a road which invited exploration. A short distance from the highway, the track plunged into a hollow that was almost always filled with water and emerged on the other side showing little evidence that many cars had passed that way. In the spring melting snows left impassable mud; during the hot summer months, dust lay thick to envelop the disturbing wheel. Ruts and rocks lurked ready to bump and bruise the undercarriage of cars if any hardy drivers decided to chance the road. In the winter the heavy snow was never plowed away and only the tracks of sleighs gave indication that anyone lived beyond the guarding belt of timber.

Yet people did live there. On a backwoods ranch in this valley my family, newly arrived from California, had settled into a determined battle with loneliness and isolation. In another land, which seemed almost another world, we had left behind a host of friends and community activities and the close fellowship of church. Our new home was eight miles from the closest neighbour and thirty miles from the nearest church; impossibly far when we had no car. No minister ever ventured near.

Season followed season and the wild country became a home. We had little money for these were Depression years. The good earth, however, brought forth abundantly all that was necessary of the staple vegetables. During the summer months we children picked buckets of wild berries to fill many a row of jars on the pantry shelf. Fish abounded in stream and lake while the woods were stocked with a never-failing supply of wild game. We sent moose and deer skins to an native village for tanning, after which we made them into vests, gloves and moccasins. When my brother and I reached school age, our mother taught us for several grades, then we enrolled in correspondence school courses.

In many ways it was a good life but one thing was lacking: the fellowship of a church. True, on Sunday mornings grandfather read the Bible and a sermon from a Christian periodical to the assembled family, and in the evening we gathered to sing familiar hymns from worn and tattered hymn books brought from the other land. Still it was not the same as a congregation united in song and worship. As much as anything we missed the friendly visits of a minister. The years went by and no minister found his way up that lonely rutted road.

One cold winter day while most of the family was away the ranch house went up in a great tower of flame and smoke. It was then that we found how false was our feeling of isolation from neighbours. Help came from near and far: food, clothing, shelter and encouragement to build again. When spring came willing hands helped to bring logs from the forest and raise again a rough but comfortable dwelling.

To family worship was added thanksgiving for new friends. But summer followed spring and changed to golden autumn and then to winter as it had done in the past and no one from any church came to visit us.

We knew that there was a minister of a similar faith in the nearest town. We knew, too, that under his care were dozens of communities spread over hundreds of square miles. We understood, but still we wished that some time he might find his way up our rutted road. He never came.

We boys grew to manhood and completed the highest grade offered through the mails. War clouds gathered and my brother went away to pilot warplanes while I stayed to help raise beef for the armies. In distant cities the airman found the fellowship of Christian people. Yet, when men put away their weapons and he returned to his home to exchange the pilots seat for a leather saddle, he found that the situation had not changed. The Church seemed as remote as ever.

Shortly after this the Rev. Stewart Crysdale came to serve the Church in that district. He was filled with an unquenchable enthusiasm and was determined to reach the remotest parts of his pastoral charge. Perhaps he drove by that rutted road many times before he noticed it, but one day he turned his car from the highway, splashed through the guarding mud-holes and followed the ruts until he turned into the gate of our outpost ranch. His friendly, open manner quickly won us over, and we were pleased when he accepted an invitation to stay with us for the night. During the evening hours he shared in family worship and led in a study of the Scriptures. When he left he promised to return . . . and did. Sometimes he brought his family and took time just to relax a few hours; always he left us with the feeling that we had regained something of the lost fellowship of the church.

Not long after this, the rising price of beef made it possible for us to exchange our buggy for a car. Shortly thereafter there was a new family at the United Church in Williams Lake—the Lees. At first we found the hymns strange and it took some time to feel a part of the congregation of town-folk, but we already knew the minister and soon we felt at home.

Stewart Crysdale was new and challenging. He spoke with contagious enthusiasm about the mission of the church and the brotherhood of man. In a way that seemed remarkedly contemporary he brought into focus the world's need for caring, conscientious people. Although up to this point my brother and I had planned to be cattlemen,the minister's words challenged us. One September we hung up chaps and spurs for the last time and went away to university. When the years of study were behind us we returned to the North that we loved, I a United Church minister, my brother a doctor to bring medical care to the far and lonely places.

With that history in mind, you can guess what happened on that warm October day. I went back to the little-used road, followed it to the yard of a weathered ranch house. With some misgivings I approached the elderly man who was splitting wood nearby.

"A minister, eh?" he remarked when I had introduced myself. "It's been a long time since one of your kind has been here. Come into the house and talk awhile."

He served me lunch and coffee so strong it made me shudder, but long after the coffee pot had cooled on the back of the stove we were still talking. He was a man of wide experience who had circled the earth and finally settled in this lonely valley. Gradually he withdrew from the world and the world did not miss him. Although it cannot be said that he agreed with all I had to say, nor I with him, we found that we shared many common beliefs. His invitation to return was warm and genuine, and as I drove away I felt that it had been well worth my while to have turned up that little rutted road.

The Long Road to Christmas

The phone rang, harsh, discordant. "If that's another choir member who can't make the choral service tomorrow night . . . !" I thought crossly, glaring at the instrument. I let it ring three times before picking it up.

"Joan here," came across the wires. I recognized the soft, urgent voice of the public health nurse and groaned inwardly; I had come to know that whenever Joan called at night some emergency was afoot. One thing I didn't need was another emergency.

The calendar had mocked me: four days left, two days . . . guiltily I found myself wishing that Christmas were over and done with.

"I'm sorry to bother you at this time of day," Joan continued, "but I have a problem and I need your help."

A snatch of a popular song flashed across my thoughts, "Don't tell me your troubles, got troubles of my own." Oh, not *great* problems, just a host of minor problems: the organist falling ill, duplicating machine broken down, change in a wedding date to the day after Christmas, extra services, people away, hampers . . . I thought of those two hampers still resting in the back seat of my car. Yes, problems like those Christmas hampers.

Love and sacrifice had gone into the preparation of the Christmas hampers. Children had saved nickels and dimes to buy small gifts. A kind grandmother, almost crippled with arthritis, had baked cakes and puddings. A young mother whose lively children filled an entire pew on Sunday morning, had found time to make boxes of delicious fudge. A local businessman had paid for a roasting chicken to put in each hamper. Finally, everything was ready and packed into boxes. When they were delivered, however, I found that two families on the list had moved away. Now I must find two more families in need and make two more trips.

"I don't mind your calling," I spoke into the telephone with a cheerfulness I really didn't feel. "How can I help you?"

Quickly she outlined her problem: a logging truck driver had brought word of a family living in a cabin at an isolated mill site. The father had hurt his leg; one of the children was ill; but they had no way of getting to town for medicine.

"I have medicine for the youngster," Joan went on, "but my car is being repaired. Could you possibly drive me out to the mill-site; you know, the one off Horsefly road?"

"But . . . but that's thirty miles," I exclaimed, "And the roads are in terrible shape after that storm last night. Couldn't the trip wait until morning?"

"I don't think so," Joan said hesitantly. "The truck driver thought the baby needed attention right away . . . perhaps I could look for someone else . . . . "

"Oh no, don't do that, I'll take you." Two hours at the very least, I thought gloomily . . . and probably another hour shovelling the car out of snow drifts, if we made it at all. Then

I felt a twinge of conscience, remembering the weariness, only partly concealed, in Joan's voice. I had nothing but admiration for the way she travelled almost impassable roads day after day, doing the dozens of tasks related to the health and welfare of children and their parents.

"I'll be right over," I said. Hanging up the phone I slipped on coat and overshoes and crossed to the manse to inform my wife of a slight change in plans. As I made my way to the garage the wind cut through my garments and the sudden chill in the air told me that it must be at least -20°F.

We talked little as I drove out on the highway and left the friendly glow of streetlights behind. Even the bright swaths cut by the headlights did not completely dispel the darkness that closed in around the car. I thought wistfully of the warm manse and the family that saw so little of me. Our three children would be decorating the tree and filling the house with excited laughter and shouts. How long had it been since I had spent an uninterrupted evening at home?

This and other troubled thoughts swarmed in my mind as I fought for control of the car on the icy highway. I felt acutely discouraged, and I should not have been depressed in the season that marked the celebration of the most Christian of all holidays: Christmas. What had gone wrong? Was it because of the frustration of having so many things to do all at once? Something was certainly dampening my Christmas spirit—of that I was sure. Thus wrapped in gloomy thoughts, I drove on in silence.

The road that led up into the hills towards the mill site was even worse than the highway. Deep, unploughed snow gripped the wheels and caused the car to slip and slide dangerously. Grimly I clung to the wheel and tramped down on the gas; the motor roared in protest and the clutch chattered.

Finally the trees opened up to reveal the mill site and we came to a stop in front of a small log cabin. I let out my breath in a sigh of relief; we had made it, but there was still the trip back.

"Here we are," said Joan cheerfully, stepping out into knee-deep snow. A barking dog bounded out to greet us, then the cabin door opened, framing a tall logger against the light. With typical north-country hospitality, he called out a welcome and an invitation to enter.

Latching the door behind us, I stood blinking in the light from a kerosene lamp, then my eyes adjusted and the interior of the cabin took shape. It was a small room with only the roughest of furniture, a double bed in one corner, an iron heater, handmade table and chairs, and a rough bench supporting a water bucket and enamel basin. At the back, a curtained doorway led off to what I guessed was another small sleeping room.

It took a moment for me to realize that there were *four* small children sleeping on the double bed, wrapped individually in blankets and plopped down like so many dumplings. Two more children were lying in a sleeping bag under the table, quiet but unsleeping, their bright eyes curiously watching our intrusion. An older child sat on the floor by the fire, while an elderly woman, who must have been in her eighties, was seated on a low stool behind the stove.

A rasping cough came from the shadows in the only remaining corner, and Joan quickly crossed the room towards the sound. "Little Eddie has such a bad chest cold." The baby's mother stood by, love and concern mirrored in her tired face as the nurse examined the child. It lay in a sagging hammock of buckskin stretched across a framework of poles.

I sat awkwardly on a plank bench and listened as the logger told me of the axe slash that had injured his leg and prevented him from working. All that he had been able to do was to keep the woodpile supplied, and that only with the help of the older children. The youngsters had set up a small evergreen and decorated it with moss, strings of red berries, and bits of tinfoil. I thought guiltily of the lights and brightly coloured balls that would now be strung on the large tree in my own cozy living room.

As we stood to leave, my eyes swept again around the room, the bare walls, the crude furniture, and the rough cupboard shelves. There were a few dishes and bowls there but scarcely any sign of food. I wondered how would this large family feed themselves over the holidays. Would there be any special Christmas treat?

Suddenly I thought of the hampers, those two unused hampers out there in the back seat of the car, and I felt a surge of excitement. *This* was why they had been left over! "Will you excuse me for a moment?" I asked. "Some of our people wanted to share at Christmas time. They've sent along a few things for you and the children."

I carried the large boxes into the cabin, thankful that there were two of them. There would be something for every child, and two chickens would not go to waste with ten to feed. Under the table two pairs of eyes grew wide with wonder as they caught a glimpse of Christmas wrappings.

We left them then, but we took with us the remembrance of a mother and father whose gratitude was expressed more in warm handclasps and misty eyes than in words, of children whose faces shone with wonder and hope, and a baby who now slept quietly in his rustic cradle.

I was surprised to notice that the frost sparkled as though the earth had been sprinkled with an infinite number of diamonds, the dark vault of the winter sky was studded with twinkling stars, and the fir trees, laden as they were with garlands of new snow, seemed freshly borrowed from an old time Christmas card. Even the road back was easy to follow now because of the tracks of the car that had gone before. What had made the change?

Then came understanding; nothing had changed but me.

Now I could see how preoccupation with my own small problems had cloaked me with self-pity, smothering the joy that could have been mine. All those others, the ones who had made the hampers possible, the public health nurse, they had found satisfaction and pleasure in helping others; now I found it too. In sharing love and compassion with this grateful family, I had gained the most.

Little Spruce Bug

A child was missing!

In any community this would capture wide attention. In a small community such as Dugan Lake, it was an unbelievable catastrophe. Everyone was involved.

Her name was Heather. Her mother had gone to Williams Lake hospital for a week leaving her nine-year-old daughter with her common-law husband, Gordon Buck. When mother returned to their cabin at Dugan Lake she was surprised that Heather was not there. Gordon explained that Heather had become upset with him two days before and had decided to walk to her great-uncle's farm a few miles down the road.

Since Heather had spent time with her uncle before, her mother was not immediately alarmed. Later that day she went to the uncle's place to pick up her daughter. Heather was not there. More than that, Heather's uncle advised that he had not seen her at all.

The R.C.M.P. were called at once. Gordon Buck appeared astounded and contrite, blaming himself for allowing Heather to go. No one searched harder than he as the woods throughout the area were combed for sign of the missing girl. She had vanished without a trace.

When several days had passed without any sign of the missing girl, police went back to Gordon Buck and questioned him intensely. They were not satisfied that he was telling the truth, but they had nothing concrete to go on. He stuck to his story that Heather had left for her uncle's farm and that he had not seen her since.

Police searched the cabin again, looking for clues they might have missed before. One thing puzzled them—a blanket with a rough circle cut out of the centre. The severed threads indicated that the cut had been made recently. Heather's mother was sure that the blanket was whole when she left for the hospital because it was one commonly used on their bed.

Pressed for an explanation, Gordon explained sheepishly that he had gone to sleep with a lighted cigarette in his fingers. He awakened to find the blanket smouldering, and had cut out the burned area to ensure that it would not reignite. To the investigating police officer, this explanation was not convincing. They began to look at Buck as a prime suspect. Still they had nothing to go on, not a single clue as to the whereabouts of the missing child.

Several small lakes were dragged without any results. The woods were searched again, as well as any sideroads along the Horsefly Road. Nothing. There was one other possibility—the mill burner. With the cooperation of the mill owner, the burner was shut down and when it had cooled, all the ashes were sifted. They found nothing that would cause them to believe the girl's body had been disposed of in this gruesome fashion.

Again the cabin was searched. Something the police

found took them back to Buck, and this time their questioning was long and intense. Buck broke down and confessed. He had raped the little girl (not for the first time) and when she screamed, he panicked and strangled her. A short time later he led the police to the spot where he had buried her body under the upturned roots of a tree.

I had followed the events of this tragedy with considerable anguish, and wished I could reach across all denominational barriers to help the family. The day that Heather's body was found I received an urgent call from the hospital. There was a very distraught man there. Could I come and see what I could do?

In the tiny hospital waiting room I found an older man who was so upset he could scarcely speak. Eventually he was able to tell me that he was the great-uncle to whom Heather was supposed to have gone. Heather had not liked Gordon Buck—for obvious reasons—and had spent more and more of her time with the uncle she loved. He had come to think of her as his own child. Her brutal murder was almost more than he could bear.

In all my years as a minister, I found the most difficult of life's emergencies to be the death of a child. That the life of a beautiful little girl should be senselessly and brutally snuffed out seemed to be the antithesis of a loving God. I agonized over this in study and prayer, but I could never find reconciliation in my mind. All that I could do was fall back on Christ's assertion about children: "Of such is the kingdom of Heaven."

Harold Kuschner in his book *Why Bad Things Happen to Good People,* struggles with this issue and does not, in my opinion, resolve it either for himself or for me. When at a later date a drunk driver snuffed out the life of my 14-year-old daughter and then sped away without stopping, I could only cry in anguish, "Why?"

A minister, in the face of stark tragedy, cannot give voice to doubt or despair. I found somewhere in the depths of my faith words of comfort to give to the grieving. Perhaps it was simply the reaching out in love that was a healing factor. I do not know. I hoped that in such times what I could say would be relevant to touch and soften human anguish.

Heather's great-uncle was anxious to meet another niece coming by plane from Winnipeg. I drove him to the airport and parked at the small terminal to await arrival of the C.P.A. flight from Vancouver. As was often the case, the flight was late. While we sat there, a police car drove up and parked beside us. Suddenly there was a cry of rage from my passenger.

"There's that murdering. . . . . . . !"

In the back seat of the police car was a handcuffed prisoner. Gordon Buck was being escorted to Oakalla Prison to await his trial. I had to physically restrain the grieving uncle from an understandable attack on the man he considered a hideous monster. Perhaps the most useful part of this incident was that Buck looked out the car window and saw face to face the anguish and rage of one of the living victims of his crime. I'm sure that visual exchange went with him to his early grave.

Over the next few days I cleared my calender of all other matters so I could devote my time to this family brought together from many places to share in the grief: mother at Deep Creek, grandmother at Soda Creek, uncle at Miocene. Each had something special to remember about Heather, "Little Spruce Bug" as she was called. Although I had never known Heather, from these deeply personal memories I was able to build a picture of a shy, happy little girl who loved the world around her and everything in it. How sadly the world had failed her!

The church was packed for Heather's funeral. There was not a dry eye in the sanctuary as we joined in the closing hymn:

> He shall gather, He shall gather,
> Bright gems for His kingdom
> Little children, little children
> Bright jewels for His crown!

In the quiet pause before the benediction, I heard a muffled cry: "My little Spruce Bug! Oh, my little Spruce Bug!"

Sleep in peace, little one, where the grass grows green, the spring flowers bloom, and the blue skies of the Cariboo smile down on your resting place.

Gordon Buck was convicted of murder in the first degree. He was the last man to be hung in B.C.

Bush Pilot

It was one of those rare September days when the blue skies of Indian summer beckon to pilots near and far. As the plane droned on, I glanced down at the clusters of ranch buildings and fields where sheep and cattle were grazing. Horsefly Lake sparkled off to my right while in the distance I identified the deep basin that held Quesnel Lake. Suddenly I spotted a twin engined plane approaching from the west, followed by another and still another.

"Williams Lake Radio, this is Golf Hotel Whisky Juliet, over Miocene. Air traffic approaching my flight path. Can you identify?"

"Hotel Whisky Juliet. Your traffic is water bombers enroute to fire in Keithley Creek area. "

As I droned over the countryside, my thoughts rambled back to a time when there were no air traffic problems in this part of the world. In fact there was only one plane in the whole of the Cariboo.

My fascination with airplanes goes back as far as I can remember. I recall, when I was four years old and living in central California, seeing an airplane flying low over our home, bound for an airshow in Sacramento. My uncle told me it was a famous plane named *Spirit of St. Louis,* and that its pilot, Charles Lindbergh, had flown all the way across the Atlantic Ocean to France. I was thrilled, and made up my mind that one day I too would be a pilot.

Shortly after, I learned that we would be moving to a remote cattle ranch far north of the Canadian border near the little town of Williams Lake. Isolated from the outside world, with not even a car or truck to drive to town, my dreams of becoming part of the world of flight seemed destined to remain just that—dreams.

During the Depression years, a single float plane flew out of Williams Lake and sometimes droned over or near our ranch. It was a bright yellow biplane with two open cockpits, one of the Moth line. We learned that a bush pilot, Barney Boe, owned it and used it to commute to his mining property at Spanish Creek, near Keithley.

On those rare occasions when Barney Boe flew over our ranch, my brother and I would race to the nearest clearing to see the yellow dot against the horizon. If we were at home we could sometimes bring the plane into focus with an ancient brass telescope. Once it was close enough for us to make out the pilot. Now *that* was a thrill.

Eventually the plane overturned on landing at Williams Lake. Fortunately neither Barney nor his passenger were injured, but the plane, when recovered from the water, was too damaged to fly again. The last time I was in the Royal British Columbia Museum at Victoria, Barney's yellow Moth was suspended in the rotunda inside the main entrance. I felt it had earned its place there, as one of British Columbia's pioneering bush planes.

While my dreams of flying remained dreams, I did cross paths with Barney Boe again. When I returned to Williams Lake as a United Church minister, Barney Boe still lived at his lakeside estate, Sidcum Place. He had given up flight, however. No longer would his plane crisscross the blue skies of the Cariboo. One day I finally met my boyhood idol, and, strangely enough, it came about as a result of parish business.

The husband in one of my church families managed to get into trouble with the law and made so poor an impression on Magistrate Poston that the parishioner was held in custody until he could post $200 cash bail—not a small sum in those days. "Not to worry," he told his wife. "Barney Boe is a good friend of mine. He'll put up the bail."

She asked me to approach Mr. Boe to enlist his assistance in freeing my hapless parishioner. I had learned that the role of minister involved many things not covered in seminary, so I was not surprised at this request. Shortly I was on my way to Sidcum Place.

Barney Boe answered my knock and invited me in, though he seemed genuinely puzzled to receive a visit from a minister. His enthusiasm for my presence was even less when I explained my mission.

"A friend of ————!" he exclaimed. "I only met *him* once—I wouldn't know him if I saw him on the street. Why would I put up money to get him out of jail?"

"I guess I was misinformed," I apologized. "I was only trying to assist his family, but I agree that it's inappropriate to ask you to put up bail if you aren't acquainted with this man." I rose to leave.

"What did you say your name was?" Barney Boe asked.

"Lee—Todd Lee. You haven't met me before either, but

your name brings back some pleasant memories." "I'm not sure I understand. Memories of what?"

"Well . . . it goes back a few years . . . " I told him about the times my brother and I would watch him fly over, and how excited we were.

"My boyhood dream was to become a bush pilot like you," I said with a smile. "It hasn't happened yet, but some day I'm going to fly. Anyway, I'm glad I had the opportunity to see you in person . . . not just as a dot in the sky."

"Well . . . " Barney Boe's face relaxed into a grin. "I hope you realize your ambition. There's nothing quite like the feeling of freedom you get when you're up there with all the world spread out below. Uh . . . just a minute."

Uncertain of what would happen next, I waited by the door until Barney Boe emerged from his den. To my surprise he handed me a cheque for $200!

"That's because of his family, not particularly for him," he said wryly. "I hope he smartens up and behaves himself."

My parishioner went free, moved away from Williams Lake and, for all I know, had no more brushes with the law. As for myself, I've never forgotten my visit with the crusty, but generous bush pilot.

Almost thirty years were to pass before my dream of flying came true, but at the age of 66 I earned my private pilot's licence. I thought it fitting that on my first cross country solo flight I should circle Sidcum Place and fly over the Knife Creek ranch where I grew up. It was here that Barney Boe, pioneer bush pilot, unknowingly kindled in the heart of a boy the will to "burst the surly bonds of earth and dance the skies on laughter-silvered wings."

On the Train to Lillooet

Bralorne—1958:

If you take a horse and pack-pony and travel southeast from Big Creek, you will cross a range of mountains and come in due course to the hilltop community of Bralorne. Here was the site of an underground gold mine that at one time rivalled Hedley's Giant Mascot mine. Bralorne is a ghost town now. Its best veins stripped of gold, the mine was closed and its shafts sealed. In 1958, however, it was a bustling mining centre with rows of neat company houses and a United Church which had a minister who had been a classmate of mine.

When it came to vacation time in the Cariboo, most people headed for the lower mainland of British Columbia. My family had different ideas. We had no love for the hectic pace of cities; those university years in Seattle and Vancouver had given us a lifetime quota of urban living. Instead, we preferred to holiday in the back-country of B.C. This summer in 1958, our goal was to explore the Bridge River Valley. As fate would have it, we had more adventure than we had planned. This adventure was to involve a train, a teen-aged native girl, and a baby that wouldn't wait. But I get ahead of myself.

We had been visiting the Bralorne minister and were getting ready to leave when our host suggested we take a scenic side trip.

"Drive over Mission Mountain to Shalath," he urged, "You'll be thrilled by that highway. When you reach Shalath, you can put your station wagon on a flat car and go up to Lillooet by train."

This was the kind of exploration we couldn't resist. I phoned for train reservations, and soon we were headed over the bumpy road to Shalath.

The highway down the east side of Mission Mountain defied superlatives. Its switch-backs were so sharp we sometimes had to back and manoeuvre to get around the corners. There were places where a skid would have launched us into open space. I shifted into low gear to take advantage of engine compression, but even so we had to stop several times to let the brakes cool.

At last we reached the foot of the mountain and breathed a sigh of relief. I stopped to ask directions from some barefoot boys fishing in a creek beside the highway.

"Could you tell me how far it is to Shalath?"

"This here is Shalath." They looked amused.

"Oh. Thank you."

Shalath amounted to a general store, a railway station, and a handful of residences. Nearby was an Indian Reserve.

The train to Lillooet consisted of a passenger coach, a small power unit, and two flat cars to carry vehicles. I drove our station wagon across shaky planks onto a flat car, then watched anxiously to see how well it would be tied down. No doubt the train crew was used to this kind of customer concern; they were careful to reassure me.

Finally we were ushered onto the train. Our three small children were excited and could hardly wait for the wheels to turn. Near us sat an elderly couple who smiled and chatted as we waited. Behind them were two bearded men who, we decided, must be prospectors. There were a handful of other passengers scattered throughout the car.

The train began to move out of the station, then came to an abrupt stop. Two more passengers climbed abroad, an older native woman and a teenage girl who was in an advanced state of pregnancy.

As soon as the latecomers were settled, the train gave a long whistle, then resumed its journey, rattling and swaying as it clicked along the tracks.

The first part of this scenic interlude was along the deep blue water of Seton Lake. In its mirrored surface was a perfect reflection of the mountains that towered above. The children were as fascinated with the ride as was I until my wife nudged me.

"I think that girl is going to have a baby," she whispered.

"Looks pretty obvious," I answered and turned back to the window.

"You misunderstood me, " Thirza persisted, "I think she's going to have a baby *now.*"

"Huh? You mean right here on the *train?*" I stole a glance at the couple across the aisle. The girl was showing unmistakable signs of discomfort and her mother a growing agitation.

"Baby! Where?" Four-year-old Patsy Ann loved babies. She looked puzzled. There were no babies on the train.

Thirza and I exchanged glances. We were both thinking

the same things: what about our young children? I tried to get their attention back to the passing scenery, but Patsy was not so easily diverted.

"What's the matter with that girl, mommy?"

"She isn't feeling good. She's going to have a baby."

"Oh . . . !" Patsy's eyes grew wide with wonder.

Thirza had reached a decision. "You take the children to the back of the coach," she instructed, "I'll see what I can do here."

Putting on her most sympathetic face, Thirza turned to the prospective grandmother. "Is there any way that I can be of help?"

"Yah . . . the baby . . . he come too soon! You know about babies?"

"Well . . . some."

"Good . . . you do it!" The older native woman rose from her seat and headed down the aisle.

"Wait . . . I'd didn't mean I'd do it *all*," Thirza protested, but the relieved woman had already found a seat at the back.

I settled the children in the farthest corner and had enlisted six year-old Kenny's help in supervising the crayons and colouring books. Then I went back to check on developments in Thirza's arena.

Contractions were only minutes apart now. The girl's eyes showed embarrassment, pain, and fear. Thirza pulled a blanket from the shelf above and spread it on the dusty floor. Then she assisted the moaning girl in lying down.

"You'll be more comfortable this way," Thirza smiled and gave the girl's hand a reassuring squeeze. Another spasm shook the young mother-to-be. She gasped and clutched Thirza's arm in a desperate grip.

"I'll go talk to the conductor—see if they can speed this thing up," I offered; I needed to do *something*.

The trainman seemed exasperated by my news.

'They always wait until the last minute," he sputtered. "Can't seem to learn!"

"Can't you go faster?" I asked, as I knew there was a hospital at Lillooet.

"Won't do any good," he shot back, "we have to go on a siding to let a freight go by. After that I'll see what I can do."

"Well—can you radio ahead, have an ambulance waiting at Lillooet?"

"Yeah, sure. I can do that."

I carried this dubious information back to Thirza. She nodded her her head.

"It probably won't matter all that much. I think she's going to deliver her baby before we get there."

Thirza turned back to her charge. The pains were coming faster now, but the girl's expression had changed. There was no embarrassment now, only fear, but beneath the fear, trust in this stranger who knelt by her side. Between them, they would bring this new life into the world.

I looked down the aisle and caught a glimpse of two dark eyes wide with excitement. Patsy was not going to miss any of this adventure. Well, perhaps this was as good a way as any for her to learn about the miracle of birth.

The freight train rumbled by, and finally we were on the move again. I could sense by the swaying and creaking of the train that the conductor had made good his promise to hurry. I willed the journey to come to an end.

The contractions and moans seemed to be matching the rhythm of the train. It couldn't be much longer. The girl was gripping Thirza's hands, the fear gone from her face. It was replaced by a blazing determination to give birth. I doubt that she was aware of anyone else but Thirza, who cheered her on with smiles and eager words of encouragement.

I felt helpless, standing there in the aisle. We males could start this process, but in the end, it was the mothers who finished the job. It had been that way since the beginning of time.

Suddenly the train whistled and the brakes went on. I swivelled my head around and was surprised to see buildings on either side of the tracks. Lillooet!

The doors flew open and two attendants rushed in with a stretcher. Moments later the moaning girl was carried out and hustled into the waiting ambulance.

We stood on the platform with our children, watching the flashing light disappear in the direction of the hospital. When it was gone, Thirza turned to me and sighed. There were tears in her eyes.

"So close, so *very* close; I wish it had come."

I squeezed her hand. I think I understood how she felt, but I must confess that I was relieved. For me, it was a heavy duty adventure, indeed.

We stopped at Lytton. I took the kids for ice cream cones while Thirza went to a nearby pay-phone. When she returned, her face was radiant. "A baby boy," she exclaimed, "seven minutes after they reached the hospital. He was *almost* my baby."

On the train to Lillooet.

Moving On

It was February, 1959, and time for decision. This was my third year with the Williams Lake Pastoral Charge. Should I stay for a fourth? Or should I be moving on?

Unlike some denominations, the United Church, except in rare cases, does not tell a minister when to move. Ordinands, placed by the Settlement Committee on first charges, are required to stay for two years. After that they are free to accept a 'call' from another congregation. I had stayed for a third year. I loved the Cariboo. I had made many good friends. The North was my home. It was not an easy decision to make.

Protocol suggested that a minister make his intentions known at the annual congregational meeting, usually in February. This gives his charge a chance to start looking for a replacement and gives the incumbent a chance to put his name on the Conference roll of ministers open for a call.

St. Andrew's had been left to the mercy of the Settlement Committee, which effectively means that it would always receive an ordinand, fresh out of seminary. It was destined to be a training ground for the inexperienced.

Still, fortune had been reasonably kind to the Cariboo. I thought back to those ministers who had gone before me: Stewart Crysdale, Gordon Hunter, Jack Colclough. Each had come from a metropolitan background to a frontier area. Each was remembered with fondness.

Any minister with grey hair will tell you that it is infinitely better to move early than to overstay one's welcome. A minister who stays on when he should move is a pain to his people and to the church. I did not want that to be my fate. I made my decision; it was time to go.

There were two factors that helped me make the decision. The first was personal: Thirza had undergone serious surgery a year before and had not fully recovered her health. Because of my unpredictable schedule, she was frequently the sole care-giver to our three lively children. The children deserved more time with their father than I was able to give. I needed a charge smaller in geographical area and closer to advanced medical services.

The second reason I chose to move was to meet the needs of the pastoral charge. It had concerns that were urgent and legitimate. Its financial situation was critical. Prior to my arrival, the Williams Lake Charge had engaged a professional fund-raising organization to assist in a building campaign. The public relations glitz that seemed to work for big city churches seemed as phony as a three-dollar bill in the Cariboo. It was a flop.

On the strength of a stack of pledges, many of which were never paid, St. Andrew borrowed the money to build a new manse and church hall. Up to the time I arrived, no payments had been made on the principal. I don't believe any were made during my term of office.

There was a hope that the coming of a young minister

who knew the North would build up the Williams Lake congregation and remedy its financial woes. I was not the man they needed for that purpose. Rightly or wrongly, I gave priority to people who were hurting, many of whom did not attend regularly or at all. I had little time or energy left over to nurture the one congregation that was responsible for the Charge's income.

When I arrived in Williams Lake in 1956, I was advised that there was $0.76 in the church treasury. Only the personal canvass of the community by a dedicated elder made it possible for me to receive my first cheque. When I left, I'm sure there was at least $10 in the bank account. Progress had been made!

One morning, an elder who had been a great support to me during my ministry, took me out for coffee and in a frank and friendly way, told me the facts of life.

"We love you; we've enjoyed your ministry; you've been good for the rural points of the district, but we're in a tough financial bind. You have a lot of strengths, but fund-raising isn't one of them. I think you know that. Todd, it's time to move on."

Far from being upset, I agreed with his appraisal of the situation and was grateful for his advice. It was time to make room for someone whose priority would be congregational nurture and fiscal renewal. Whether there would be such a person among the year's crop of ordinands would be the Settlement Committee's problem. My successor, Art Anderson, was better suited to this task.

My remaining four months were spent in a final visitation to all the wonderful people I had come to know in the vast reaches of the Cariboo. It was a wistful time for me. I had ridden their horses, milked their cows, celebrated with them in joy, wept with them in sorrow. Their sons and daughters had come to me to be married and brought new babies to be baptized. On sunny slopes above ranch houses, where family members had turned the sod, I had stood with grieving family to lay loved ones to rest, some gone before they had time to live. This was the land of my childhood. These were my kind of people. It was hard to go.

The last good-byes had been said, the movers had come and gone. We were packed to leave for a two-week holiday at Bella Coola before taking up new duties on Vancouver Island.

"Mommy, I don't feel good," our five-year-old Patsy whimpered. She was warm. . . too warm. A cool bath might help.

"Todd, come and see," Thirza called from the bathroom. Patsy's back and stomach were covered with a rash. Measles!

We held a hasty conference. Camping in Bella Coola was definitely out. Next, there was a long distance call to Nanaimo. Yes, we could start our ministry a month early and take our holidays later. My mother in Mission assured us that we were welcome to stay on the way over, measles and all.

We decided that the children—Ron had broken out too—would be more comfortable travelling at night than in bright sunlight. We would leave at dusk on the eight-hour trip to the lower mainland. While Thirza fed the children and made them as comfortable as possible, I busied myself with last minute loading details. We would not need our camping-out gear after all.

Two men found me tying down the cover of the trailer. I knew before they spoke that these two had been celebrating, or, as it turned out, drowning their sorrows.

"Mr., you're the United Church minister, aren't you?"

I hesitated for a moment. Technically I wasn't—but it didn't appear to be a time for technicalities. I nodded my head.

"My friend here belongs to your church. He needs your help."

"Oh. Okay." Perhaps he had been baptized in St. Andrews, but I'd never seen him within its walls since I had been there. That wasn't a problem, though; I'd never considered church membership to be important when someone was hurting.

"Can you tell me what the problem is?" I asked the second man who had not yet spoken.

Suddenly, it was as though a dam had broken letting sorrow and anger pour out. He and his wife had a good life, worked hard, played hard, raised their kids, and relaxed in the Lakeview bar on a Saturday night. Then his wife started going to another church in town. Everything changed. No more drinking, no more smoking, no more 'Cariboo' language. As a husband, he no longer measured up. His marriage was in shambles—and it was all the fault of that #/%@# pastor!

"I'm really sorry about your marriage," I sympathized, "how can I help you?"

"You can go over there tomorrow and punch that pastor's lights out!"

"Look," I said, "it's really hard to solve problems when you've had too much to drink. Why don't you sleep on it and try again tomorrow when you're sober?"

"Huh?"

"Yeah," said his friend, "that's pretty good advice. Thanks, Rev. See you tomorrow."

I sighed and turned back to my trailer. Then there flashed

into my mind a headline the local paper might have used:

LOCAL CLERICS SLUG IT OUT AT HIGH NOON

In spite of myself, I broke into a grin. There were some things about the Cariboo that never changed!